L.I.F.T.

A Coach Approach to Parenting

KATE ARMS

ISBN: 978-1-9994302-7-6

CONTENTS

ACKNOWLEDGMENTS

The ideas in this book are inspired by many teachers. I am especially grateful to Phil Porter and Cynthia Winton-Henry, founders of InterPlay, for introducing me to principles that undergird all my work; all the InterPlay leaders who have helped shape my understanding of inner authority; Celia Swanson for introducing me to Co-Active coaching; all my Co-Active coaching and leadership teachers and classmates; all my Organization and Relationship Systems Coaching (ORSC) teachers and classmates; the Impalas, with whom I refined many of these ideas; Jen Merrill and Chris Wells, who gave me the first opportunity to present these ideas publicly; Corey Reid for helping me take all the ideas and turn them into a unified framework, and Lenore Butcher and Kate Nachman for their feedback on the manuscript.
A deep thank you also to all the parents who have taken my classes, worked with me as coaching clients, spoken to me at conferences, and connected with me in person and online. Without your enthusiasm and willingness to put these ideas into practice and share your experience with me, this book would never have come to be.

INTRODUCTION

None of us come to parenting with training or experience.

We have memories of how we were raised and expectations we have gleaned from our families, our communities, and the media. Most of us have some mix of things from our childhood that we remember fondly and want to recreate and other things we have sworn we would never repeat with our own kids. If we are partnered, our partner has a different set of expectations, dreams, and avoidances. The bulk of our ideas about parenting are gut feelings rather than explicit knowledge.

Our parents probably didn't show us how they decided how to parent us. We learned through experiencing the impact of their choices.

We were raised by generations who lived in a different world than we are facing. The late 20th and early 21st centuries have seen rapid cultural changes about family structures and gender roles and economic changes brought about by social changes and technological innovation. We know that the world we were raised for is not the world we are living in, and we know that the world our children will be facing is unlike anything we have known.

We know that we must prepare our children for the

uncertainty of the gig economy, a lifetime of self-directed learning, diverse environments, wicked global challenges, and rapid technological shifts. We don't know whether to embrace or reject the technology they are surrounded by.

We need new models of parenting that address the needs of this new world.

Many of us have an intuitive understanding that teaching our children to mindlessly obey authority, even our own as their parents, will not help them succeed in this new world, but we do not have alternative models for teaching cooperation, respect, and responsibility. Many of us struggle to find a middle ground between authoritarianism and overly permissive parenting.

The L.I.F.T. framework is designed specifically to provide such an alternative model. It is grounded partially in the long-term development approaches of youth sports coaching and partially in the principles of empowering leadership that have been developed in innovative companies and form the cutting edge of corporate leadership training.

Youth athletic coaching includes awareness of natural childhood development and ways of teaching that work with developing children. Modern corporate leadership models are designed to develop employees who learn on the job, are flexible and collaborative, and are enthusiastic and effective contributors. Together, these two bodies of work contain a treasure trove of material that can help parents.

When asked about their goals, parents are remarkably consistent. Everybody wants their kids to grow up to be happy and successful. Most also want them to fit into a moral framework that their parents approve of.

Children also want to be happy and successful. However, they frequently disagree with their parents about what they think will make them happy.

And everybody struggles with the reality that sometimes success and happiness seem to be mutually exclusive.

In developing this approach, therefore, I have made several basic assumptions. I assume that parents want their children to grow up to feel good about their lives and be capable of taking care of their financial needs. I assume that parents hope their adult children will want to come home to visit out of a genuine desire to connect with their parents and not merely from a sense of obligation. I assume that children fundamentally want the same thing.

I assume that parents and children want family to be communities of love, belonging, mutual joy, and support, and that conflict is inevitable and must be navigated.

The L.I.F.T. approach offers tools for conducting the conversations about happiness and success that are required for parents and children to understand each other, build strong and loving relationships, and prepare children for adulthood.

At first glance, the four-part L.I.F.T. approach may seem backwards. That is because it is focused on relationship first and teaching last. Without the foundational elements of a safe and trusting relationship, our children do not learn effectively.

Most approaches to solving parenting programs assume a loving relationship and directly address the challenge of getting children to do the thing adults expect and want them to do. Unfortunately, many of the techniques they teach inadvertently damage the underlying relationship. The L.I.F.T. approach is designed specifically to avoid tactics that undermine the parent-child bond.

Many parents are focused primarily on the things children do not yet know and are weighed down by the responsibility of passing on all those skills. This responsibility is stressful, and the stress interferes with our ability to love our children fully as they are in this moment.

Under stress, we forget a fundamental fact about learning. Learning is inherently stressful and happens best when children have access to their most creative selves.

The L.I.F.T. framework relieves some of that stress.

The L.I.F.T. framework consists of four foundational principles and four stages of coaching.

Foundations. The four guiding principles of L.I.F.T. are: 1) children are naturally creative, resourceful, and whole; 2) successful parenting is focused on the whole child; 3) build from what exists right now; and 4) children develop on their own timelines.

Stage 1: Listen to Learn. Children are undeveloped, unskilled, and lacking knowledge, but they are not born as blank slates. Learning to listen well to what is said and unsaid helps us learn about our children in ways that help us help them.

Stage 2: Inspire. The coach approach to motivation is to inspire through love rather than fear and to encourage enlightened self-interest.

Stage 3: Facilitate. We cannot do the work of learning and growing for our children. By accepting this reality, we can embrace our roles as facilitators and catalysts for growth and development and give our children responsibility for their part in the process.

Stage 4: Teach. As adults, we know many things that our children will benefit from knowing. This section of the framework addresses effective ways of passing that information on.

The foundations form the attitude or approach to the stages. The first three stages of coaching form a spiral of growing strength, starting in order and evolving into a toolkit that you can draw on as necessary. The fourth stage, Teach, is a specific application of Facilitate that comes into play when adults have skills and expertise that children want and are ready to learn from them.

Before our children can benefit from our attempts to teach them, we must have listened to them to learn what they want to do, inspired them to face the challenges inherent in learning, and facilitated their self-directed learning such that they have identified the need to be helped in their endeavors to learn what they want to know.

Facilitating their learning is the heart of the coach approach to parenting. Therefore, there are more tools in that section of the book than in any other. These tools are grouped into three elements of facilitation: goal setting, implementing, and reassessing.

Together, the four stages and the foundations allocate responsibility between parents and children and offer guidance to parents about when to step in and when to leave children to their own processes.

The L.I.F.T. framework is a coach-approach to parenting and is part of a bigger model of family leadership that includes co-parenting kids and a coaching-based leadership approach to running a household. The focus of this portion of the model is creating nurturing relationships that powerfully support children becoming happy and successful adults. The quality of relationship created through a coach approach to parenting is a powerful support for effectively running a household, supporting educational endeavors, and teaching life skills, but specific advice on those tasks is beyond the scope of the framework as presented in this book. Some general ideas on how to use the framework will be presented in the chapter on Family Matters.

My hope is that this approach to parenting will help you build strong, loving relationships with your children as you help them navigate the complexities of life and prepare for their adult lives. I believe that the quality of relationship that is achieved through a coach approach is the foundation for long-term family harmony, enjoyable work cultures, and greater peace in the wider community. These are lofty goals, I admit. I have seen so many profound shifts in families and organizations when they start applying these principles that I do not believe they are unreasonable.

I believe that implementing the ideas in the following chapters will help you create deep intimacy and a nurturing sense of belonging in your family as you do the hard work of raising the next generation.

So, let's get started.

FOUNDATIONS

Four basic principles serve as foundations for the L.I.F.T. framework. Think of them as supporting the entire approach. Together they form a way of seeing the process of parenting that will allow you to be coachlike with creativity in the face of whatever arises.

If you forget the other specifics of the L.I.F.T. framework but parent from the foundations, you will be building a relationship that can stand strong and will support your children, even if it doesn't look quite like anybody else's relationships.

I often speak of parenting as building in earthquake territory. We are working with our children to create their adulthoods. But the materials we are working with are constantly changing.

Most obviously, our children are developing rapidly. The natural processes of child development are driven by biology that even the experts do not fully understand. But one thing we do know is that child development is a complex product of innate processes, genetic material, the environment, and children's unique experiences.

Perhaps less obviously, we are also constantly changing.

As adults, we tend to think of ourselves as in some ways fully formed, but we are still learning and growing, both through continued natural development and through encountering new experiences.

The world around us is also continuing to shift and change. Political changes. Cultural shifts. Technological developments. Births and deaths in the family and neighborhood. Major stress is a fact of life.

Earthquakes put major stress on buildings. Building practices in earthquake territory counter the stress through some combination of flexible foundations, shock absorption, reinforcements, and technologies that reduce the amount of stress that actually impacts the building.

In the same way, the foundations of the L.I.F.T. framework provide moderating forces, flexibility, and shock absorption in parenting relationships. When everything else is moving, these four principles will keep things manageable.

Children are Naturally Creative, Resourceful, and Whole

Assuming that children are naturally creative, resourceful, and whole respects them as individuals separate from us. It also allows us to give them responsibility for what they can be responsible for. It is the foundation for the letting go that we spend their childhood preparing for and practicing.

Children are clever, sometimes too clever for the comfort of the adults around them. They find ways to meet their needs. The younger they are, the fewer skills they have. But the human brain is a highly skilled learning device.

Their first need is to make sure their parents or other adults take care of them until they are capable of taking care of themselves. As infants, children apply all their resources to making that happen.

Their second need is to become self-reliant. This need arises naturally in response to the inevitable times that adults disappoint them and to learning that we will die. We can trust that our children have no desire to remain dependent on us forever.

Making tools is a natural human capability. Finding and using resources comes naturally to kids. The youngest babies are exploring their world and figuring out how to use the resources available to achieve their goals.

As parents, assuming that our children are naturally resourceful and creative gives us options. We can provide information and make our children aware of available resources and let them figure out how to use them.

If we also assume that our children are whole, we create a strong foundation for our relationship with them and a great foundation for their long-term mental health.

Carl Rogers, the humanistic psychologist, talked about unconditional positive regard as the foundation of a nurturing relationship. Unconditional positive regard is not acceptance of everything that someone does. It is more subtle and more powerful.

To see someone with unconditional positive regard is to believe that they are human beings with agency, capable of choosing how to respond to any situation. It is to believe that, at any given moment, they are doing the best they can.

The theory rests on the belief that people have innate desires to be socially constructive, people also have a need for self-determination, and the more the need for self-determination is honored, the more the urge to be socially constructive will take hold.

If we as parents wish to raise children to be socially responsible adults, therefore, we should focus our efforts on honoring our children's need for self-determination in order to stimulate their innate desires to be productive members of society. Coaching is a way of supporting people that deeply honors their need for self-determination.

Seeing a child with unconditional regard is to look for how their self-sabotage and challenging behaviors are the best that they can do at the time. It is to see them as resourceful, creative, and whole even when they are lacking skills, motivation, or understanding.

This is a radical departure from many parenting approaches. Many parents hear this and wonder how they will ever get their children to behave if they see them as always doing their best. How will they be able to hold high expectations if they condone bad behavior? But seeing your children as naturally creative, resourceful, and whole does not mean that you see their behavior as ideal.

What it does mean is that discipline has to change. Discipline can no longer focus on punishing undesirable behavior. Discipline has to look at why this particular behavior was the best the child could do at the moment. Was too much expected of them? Were they tired, hungry, sick or otherwise not at their best? Was there something else that was motivating them more? What need were they trying to satisfy?

Discipline becomes about learning from mistakes, deliberate practice, deeper understanding, and growing resiliency.

The primary impacts of seeing our children as naturally creative, resourceful and whole are: 1) they feel seen and respected for who they are and not what they do, and 2) we like them more. From this foundation, adults and children build the kind of relationship that supports learning and growth.

Think about it. If you see your child as broken and willfully misbehaving, how will you treat them? How would you react to being treated that way? If you see your child as doing their best, what would be different? How would you behave differently? How would you respond to being treated that way?

It is not easy to make this shift if the culture around you expects you to keep your child in line and punishes you for their immaturity. You will be called on to put your commitment to a healthy relationship with your child before your image.

You will have to be willing to share control of the relationship with your child and follow their lead sometimes. You will need to become comfortable with how they are different from what you imagined, expected, or wanted in and for your children. You will need to start letting them grow up and be responsible for their own lives earlier than you imagined.

The rewards will include a more intimate knowledge of and appreciation for the unique miracle that is this child. It is likely that you will also be the recipient of more spontaneous expressions of love from children at ages where many children are fighting to become independent.

What I have seen over and over is that parents who stop trying to control their children when they are young and learn to coach them have more fun parenting teens. If the teens are already confident that they are not extensions of their parents, they don't have to fight to prove it. And parents get the benefit of gentler relationships with their nearly adult children as they muddle their way through adolescence.

Please note that treating your child as whole is possible even if they suffer from a disability, mental illness, or the like. The wholeness of your child includes their challenges. Your child's weaknesses and difficulties are part of how they experience and navigate the world. Of course, the specific challenges your child faces will have an impact on the kind of support you need to offer them. The important thing is that they are who they are, and they need help navigating the world as themselves.

Successful Parenting Focuses on the Whole Child

Children are minds, bodies, emotions, spirits, academics, activities, siblings, friends, and more. A coach approach to parenting recognizes that these elements of the child must all be attended to.

If we focus only on academics, how will they learn to be kind? If we focus only on athletics, how will they learn to drive? If we focus only on doing chores, how will their emotions develop?

If we honor the wholeness of our children, they will learn how to honor that wholeness for themselves.

Think of your experience as a child. What parts of you did not get supported by your parents? What might have been different if that part of you had been included?

If we had some part of ourselves excluded by our families of origin, we may be tempted to over-focus on including that part of our children or we may exclude it similarly. Focus on the whole child reminds us to look for harmony and balance in the elements of our child that we are nurturing.

Focusing on the whole child also includes focusing on the harmonies between home, school, friends, sports, art, unstructured play, and screen time.

Just like adults, children have five elements of their lives that must be fulfilling in order for them to prosper. They must have: 1) sufficient positive emotional experiences to balance out the rough times; 2) a sense of agency and self-determination; 3) a sense that they matter and what they do has an impact; 4) a sense of accomplishment; and 5) good relationships with friends and family.

In a coach approach to parenting, we focus on these psychological needs first and then help them see how health, hygiene, chores, academics, sports, etc. can serve to meet those needs.

We Must Build from What Exists Right Now

The only moment that we ever experience is THIS moment. Everything happens NOW.

Staying aware of what is happening right now is very hard for parents. We know that we have only a few years to prepare our children for life after they leave home. We have forgotten how unformed we were when we left school, or we remember and wish for our children to be better prepared. We want to save them from the heartaches we suffered.

We want to be able to look back and say that we did a good job as parents. We worry that our children will suffer a life of misery and destitution if we fail. (Do you see how seeing or children as naturally creative, resourceful, and whole might help us out here? They will find ways to manage despite our failures.)

At the same time, our children are developing fast and unpredictably. We remember how they were yesterday and are taken aback when today they are taller or more competent. Many parents consistently feel like they have finally figured out how to parent the child they had six months ago.

We frequently misremember our own childhoods. We look to averages and other kids to see what our kids should be capable of. We worry that this one kid has a problem because although they are advanced in math and great at keeping a room tidy, the dishes they wash are never really clean, their emotional reactivity is still high, and they seem to have missed the boat on the need to flush.

In THIS moment, there is a child who exists as they are, a parent (you) who is having a particular experience, and a circumstance that must be dealt with. The more you can be in this moment, seeing what is going on right now, the more you will be able to lead towards the future you want to create with your child.

You have dreams for the future and ideas for what will help you get there. But all you can do right now is take one step. What is the next step?

You will almost certainly find that as your children develop, the goals and dreams that you had for them diverge from the goals and dreams they have for themselves. Even more challenging, as they develop, your children will change their minds about their own goals, often just after you invested time or money into helping them pursue the goal they are abandoning. You must learn to hold goals lightly and reassess them in light of what you learn now, and now, and now.

The way to deal with the fact that you, your children, and the world are changing is to keep checking in and noticing what is happening right now. Have present circumstances shifted in a way that suggest that the direction of the next step should be reassessed?

Your children are the age they are, with the skills they currently have, and they can only grow up one minute at a time. See where they are now and help them take the next step in a direction that makes sense. Then take the next step from there. When you look back together, you will see the path that you have walked together and the life that you have helped them create.

Children Develop on Their Own Timelines

This one can be hard to accept, especially when our children's developmental patterns don't fit the normal expectations. Please note that normal is a setting on a dryer. No child develops in lock step with statistical norms. Your child is no exception.

We cannot control the speed at which our children develop.

The saying "when the student is ready, the teacher appears" is usually read from the student's perspective.

When you are ready for a stage of growth, learning, or development, you will notice the opportunity to learn it in something that already exists around you. You can see everyone as your teacher, and you will learn whatever lesson you are ready for from them. This can be reassuring and empowering as a student.

From the parent's perspective, however, it is humbling. When your child is ready for a lesson that you can see they need to learn, they will find a teacher. However, that teacher may not be you. And they will be ready when they are ready, not a moment before. You can be a catalyst for their learning, but you cannot make them learn.

You will constantly be surprised by their developmental timing and where they find their lessons.

When you accept their time tables and hold strong in your belief that they will find their way, several positive things occur. They feel safe and loved for exactly who they are. They can borrow your belief that they will succeed when they are feeling incompetent. You will feel ease about where they are right now.

How to Use These Foundations

These foundations are attitudes for you to cultivate, beliefs for you to stand on.

When you interact with your child from these assumptions, your love and respect for them will shine through every specific action that you take.

Without these foundations, you may find yourself inadvertently teaching them that they are not worthy of love, not enough, or somehow fundamentally broken.

You know that what you want for your children is their happiness and success in life. You know that you have more experience of the world and more knowledge of what that will require than they do. You know that you are responsible for creating a family setting that nurtures them.

You know that a bad family situation can create harm that lasts a lifetime. You care.

You care very deeply.

This caring creates pressure. Pressure that can push us into fear-based parenting as opposed to love-based parenting. These foundations keep us coming from love and give us principles we can return to and bolster our own courage when we feel ourselves acting out of fear.

Everything that follows in the rest of the model works because of the foundations. Without these foundational attitudes, everything else will come across as an attempt to mold our children into who we want them to be. With these foundations in place, everything we do, however unskillful, is a vehicle for our love and nurturing spirits to work in service of our children's happiness.

This book contains very few detailed examples and scripts. This is intentional. There are dangers in being given too much detail about what to do in a given situation. No situation is ever exactly the same as an example. If you follow a script, it is harder to react to what is happening in the moment. Really good actors pull it off when they have had enough rehearsal, and they are working in a very limited world with other actors who have learned their lines. Your children will not play their parts exactly as written.

More importantly, however, children are very good at listening for our intentions and what isn't being said. They pay more attention to deciphering what we really want than to what we say. We cannot hide behind our words. On the up side, this means that if we have the right attitude and intention, the exact words we use don't matter. Hopefully, you will find this reassuring.

If you find yourself faltering in these beliefs, be gentle with yourself. Notice that you have fallen off this path, let it be, and begin again.

Frequent reminders that you want to stand on these foundations are powerful. You might want to post notes on your bathroom mirror, set reminders in your phone, or have a reflective journaling practice while you are starting to embrace this approach. Something as simple as writing your thoughts about these principles for five minutes each morning will eventually make them part of how you look at the world.

The most powerful shock absorbers for the tectonic shaking that is an inevitable part of parenting are these four foundational principles: children are naturally creative, resourceful, and whole; successful parenting focuses on the whole child; we must build from what exists right now; and children develop on their own timelines. With them in place, we can shift to the first building technology, Listen to Learn.

STAGE ONE: LISTEN TO LEARN

The first stage in the L.I.F.T. model is Listen to Learn. Listening is such a foundational part of life that it is hard to be an adult and admit that we might not be good at listening. And yet, very few people are taught how to listen well as children. It should come as no surprise that most of us get to adulthood with some bad habits and some weak skills.

When we learn to listen well, we change the quality of our relationships dramatically. When we listen to our children well, we learn who they are, what matters to them, and who they are trying to become. We learn how we can support them.

Without listening, we are only guessing about who our children are and what flourishing will look and feel like to them. We are only guessing at what will be best for them. And, unfortunately, most of the time we will guess wrong. Over time, if we create an environment where they feel safe revealing themselves to us, we will become more and more accurate in our guesses. Even so, we will always miss things that feel important to our children.

Maintaining a practice of listening to our children to learn who they are in this moment helps create an environment where they feel safe and helps us know how we can support them as they develop into happy and successful adults.

You may have encountered active listening, which is the most commonly taught listening skill, but there is more to listening well than active listening. If you haven't heard of active listening, don't worry. I will discuss it a little later.

When we are listening, we have to choose what we focus on. We can focus on ourselves, the impact that what we are hearing is having on us, and how we are going to respond. We can focus on the content of what the other person is saying. Or, we can focus on the things that are going on around and behind the words that are being spoken.

Focus on Ourselves

Being able to focus on ourselves is important for understanding ourselves, for noticing when our values and boundaries have been breached, for practicing wise self-care, and sometimes for connecting with our intuitive reactions to things that we cannot easily articulate.

If we are focused solely on ourselves, however, we miss much of what other people are saying. The words they say become information that we use to relate to ourselves. They cease to be a vehicle for communication.

When we focus on ourselves, we often start formulating our response to what is being said before the other person has finished speaking. We assume that we know what they are going to say and formulate our rebuttal without letting ourselves be influenced. It is a form of defense.

As parents, it is tempting to not listen when our children want something that will inconvenience us or that is against our values or challenges our sense of identity or priorities. It is easy to hear them beginning to ask for something they want and immediately start formulating our argument for why they shouldn't want it or why they can't have it.

When we do that, we miss an opportunity to build relationships with our children. And we miss an opportunity to learn more about who they are.

In order to listen and learn, we must dampen our initial responses and get curious about what our child saying. What is really important to them? What is it about who they are that has prompted them to share this? What are they showing us about who they are and who they want to be?

We cannot build healthy relationships with our children if we are entirely focused on ourselves. And we cannot have a healthy relationship with ourselves without ever focusing on ourselves.

In coaching, we try to keep a light touch on our focus on ourselves and shift more of our focus to the other areas.

Focus on the Content

When you listen to focus on the content, you are listening with a hard focus on the person in front of you and what they are saying. You are listening to understand what the words they are saying mean and how the tone of their voice suggests you should interpret it.

This is the kind of listening that most people are talking about when they talk about the listening portion of active listening.

Active listening is the process of listening intently to the content of what people are saying and checking to make sure that you understood it. You listen, paraphrase what you heard, and ask if that was what the other person meant. And you do have to use your own words when you paraphrase. Simply repeating their words back to them doesn't help you confirm that you understand, and it will probably annoy them.

As your children get older, you will want to be able to paraphrase what you thought they said so that you can check for comprehension. When they are young, however, they may not have the breadth of vocabulary to confirm your understanding in this way.

When people first start practicing active listening, they are often surprised by how hard it is to do well. If you aren't genuinely trying to understand the other person, active listening feels patronizing. You can't fake curiosity. It has to be genuine.

In addition, it turns out that paraphrasing is hard. No two people use words the same way. We learn what words mean in context. Each word accumulates meaning that includes all the contexts in which we have encountered that word. Our history of contexts is unique to us. What we think words mean is slightly different than any one else does. Subtle distinctions in how we understand words can create huge misunderstandings between people.

This is especially true in English because English has so many words with synonyms borrowed from other languages. When we learn words, our brains make distinctions between synonyms because our brain assumes that different words have different meanings. Our distinctions are likely to be different from other people's distinctions.

Think of the words compassion, pity, and empathy. I am sure you have a gut feeling about the differences between them. But are you sure everyone would use compassion the way you do? I have a friend who uses compassion to describe what I call pity and empathy to describe what I call compassion. In certain conversations, we get into difficulty because we forget this about each other. The confirmation step in active listening helps us discover these differences so that we can deal with them.

It is useful to remember that people misunderstand

each other far more than they think. The more precisely people use language, the more this tends to be true among adults. Children often use words more generally or more specifically than adults. Confirming that you understand what they are trying to say can reveal useful information in addition to helping them feel valued and seen.

Listening for content manages the bulk of the objective, factual content of a conversation, but often very little of the relational and emotional information. For that, we need the third kind of listening.

Focus on the Context

The third kind of listening is listening with a focus on the broader context. This can feel a little vague and fuzzy at first, but parents are typically already doing a lot of this. You are paying attention to all the nonverbal, contextual things that are also present when you are talking with your children. What are they not saying? What is their body language saying? How do the power dynamics in the conversation affect what they say? Are you sensing that they are ashamed or avoiding something?

Parents listen to pre-verbal children this way all the time. When a baby cries, parents observe the situation to try and understand why the child is upset. Is it a long time since they slept or ate? Is there a loud noise in the area? Were they just startled by the dog?

As children learn to talk fluently, parents tend to slowly shift to a greater focus on the content of what their children say. The closer to adult fluency children get, the easier it is to let the balance between listening for content and listening for the context behind and around the content slide too far to listening for content.

When we hear the things that aren't being said and notice how the environment is affecting what is said, sharing what we observe with our children can help them feel heard and seen more fully than if we simply focus on the words that they say.

One thing we need to remember when we are listening for these elements is that we are sometimes using our intuition more than our rational minds. When we get a sense that something is not being said but don't have specific facts to point to in order to name it for ourselves and our children, we should make it clear that we are guessing a little.

Instead of saying, "you aren't telling me everything," try saying, "you seem less sure than sometimes, as though maybe you aren't telling me everything. Is there something else?" Notice that "is there something else?" doesn't make any guesses about what the something else might be, just that there might be something else. The more open-ended the question that we use to check out whether our intuition is right or not, the more likely we will nudge them to share what else is going on.

Where to Focus

A coaching perspective to listening involves mostly listening to the content and the context. A small amount of attention on ourselves may help us to notice our intuitive awareness but more than a little interferes with our ability to hear our children fully.

We can listen fully to our children and then check in with our own reactions before responding. We do not have to listen to our response while we are trying to listen to our children. Our response will still be there when they have finished speaking, though it may not be exactly the same response we would have made if we had interrupted them.

If you want to test that theory, try this voice mirroring exercise. While someone is speaking, use the voice inside your head to repeat what they are saying as close to when they say it as possible. When they finish speaking, start responding without taking the time to decide what you are going to say. Notice whether or not you have something to say.

Learning to put all of our focus on our children, then listening to ourselves, and then responding helps us get a deeper understanding of our children and builds the trust that comes from having been truly heard.

In general, the more emotionally charged a conversation is, the more you want to be listening to the context, with less attention on the exact words and almost no attention on your own reaction. You should then notice your reaction before you speak. This process will allow you to hear your child more fully and allow you to choose how you react more carefully.

Self-Management

Listening like this requires self-management. You will probably find yourself wondering how you can be the parent if you aren't ahead of the game. At times, you will be caught up wondering whether you are going to need to be a disciplinarian or a comforter. Other times, your children will be saying things that irritate you or remind you of things you don't want to think about. They may even trigger horrible memories of your own childhood.

It is your job as the parent-coach to keep the focus on them as you listen to them.

You will need to learn to trust that answers will come when it is your time to speak, that silence while you compose your thoughts is not a problem, that asking for a moment to think about it is acceptable, and probably other things.

What interferes with your ability to put the focus fully on your children will be slightly different than anybody else's. If you look closely, however, you will almost certainly find a fear or sense of threat hiding behind intrusive thoughts about yourself.

To get better at self- management, get curious about the fears that are lurking behind your impulse to craft a response instead of listening. When you understand your fears, you can develop ways of minimizing the risk that those fears will be realized.

For example, if your daughter wants to buy a new video game that you have never heard of and she is pressuring you to make a decision now, you might be afraid of making a poor decision. You might allow her to buy a game that turns out to have inappropriate material. Or, you might deprive her of a really excellent game that has a social component and teaches something you want her to learn. If you know that you are afraid of making a bad decision, rather than coming up with a hurried and defensive answer while she is talking, you can be transparent with her and buy yourself some time by hearing her fully, then saying, "I hear that you really want this game and I can feel the pressure that you feel for me to make a decision right now. I don't like making decisions while I feel pressured because I know I don't make good decisions under pressure without more information than I have right now. I need time to think about it."

You may find that just saying that calms you down enough that you can think more clearly immediately. Or you may find that you still need more time. Either way, listening to her fully will help her feel heard. Being heard makes it more likely that she will be willing to accept a delay.

Curiosity

Listening to learn about your child requires curiosity. You need to actively cultivate curiosity about this special human being in front of you. Remember that they are constantly growing and developing. There are many things about them that you genuinely do not know. Listening to learn requires that you actively try to discover what you do not know about them.

It is easy for parents to parent the child we remember from six months ago as opposed to the child that is currently in front of us. We need to take time to discover who is here with us now.

This is not something you can fake. It isn't just about asking questions, though asking questions is a natural response to genuine curiosity.

Children are clever and intuitive. Their survival depends on figuring out how their parents tick so they can get what they need from them. If we pretend to be curious about our children, they will know.

It can be hard to remember to be curious about our children when we are under pressure to get lots of things done or they are challenging us. Start by focusing on your curiosity about them during slow or fun times. Watch them playing and wonder what they are thinking. See them doing their homework and wonder how they feel when they are struggling. Develop the habit of cultivating your curiosity by practicing in low stress situations and it will become more likely to spontaneously arise under pressure.

Listen to Their Emotions

Learning to handle emotions is hard for children. They first need to learn to be aware of emotions and discover that they can notice them and be separate from them. You can help by listening to and for their emotions and teaching them to listen to their own emotions.

Then, when they are able to listen to their emotions and name them for you, you can ask questions about their emotions directly.

Listening to learn helps us know our children well

enough to start the process of helping them identify their goals. It helps us to avoid the trap of molding them to meet our goals.

We will need to keep listening to learn throughout our parenting journey as our children grow and develop. This practice will continue to serve us as parents of adult children as we navigate the changes that come as they cease to depend on us for their physical survival.

Before we can help our children set and meet specific goals, we must make sure they are ready to learn, and motivated and hopeful enough to be willing to endure the stresses of learning and development. Therefore, the next stage of L.I.F.T focuses on cultivating motivation and hope.

STAGE TWO: INSPIRE

The second stage of the L.I.F.T. approach is to Inspire. Inspiration is the process of increasing motivation. Our children have intrinsic motivation to learn when they are born, and they continue learning rapidly and continually unless we get in their way.

Like adults, however, they will go through inevitable periods of struggling to learn or avoiding things that they know are hard.

As parents, part of our job is to help them remain optimistic and encouraged about their ability to learn even when they are having a hard time.

Human beings have a negativity bias. We respond more strongly to negative sensations and experiences than we do to positive ones. This is undoubtedly useful in many situations. We do not want our children to be burned several times before they learn that fire is hot. Of course, we would really prefer that our children never be burned at all. The truth is that even though we may put our hand close to a fire and get close enough that we sense that any closer would be too hot, there is nothing like getting a slight burn from a match or an oven rack to teach us that too much heat really is a bad thing. Our children need negative experiences to learn. But not too many.

One of the difficulties of childhood is that everything is new. More new things are thrown at children every day. We send our children to school and tell them that their job is to learn. We are also constantly teaching them new things at home. But we forget that learning is stressful.

Think about the first few weeks in a new job. The first day you may be shown around, introduced to people, helped to learn a few simple things, and asked to fill out paperwork with information you already know. It is relatively easy, exciting, and you have someone helping you through. Soon, though, you have been shown everything once, people think you know everything you need to know, and you are treated as though you know everything. For a while, you are lost. Slowly, you figure out what needs to go where, who really has what information, and which people say one thing and mean another. After a couple of years in the job, you come in to work, know exactly what to do, do a good job, and go home satisfied that you did what you had to do.

Children spend most of their lives in the "you are lost" phase. Each time they think they have something figured out, and often substantially before they hit that stage, they are given three new things they are expected to learn and have one experience that their prior experiences haven't prepared them for. This is a very stressful way to live. The stress of learning is why learning through play is vital for children.

Play reduces the stress and increases motivation and willingness to keep learning. But, and this is crucial, the kind of play that reduces stress is not necessarily the kind of play kids get in organized sports.

The kind of play that reduces stress and increases motivation is purposeless, all-consuming, and fun, as described by Stuart Brown in his book *Play: How it Shapes the Brain, Opens the Imagination, and Invigorates the Soul.*

Parents throughout time have found ways to make chores as playful as possible. The inspiration element of L.I.F.T. taps into that impulse and goes a little further.

Inspiration reminds children of who they are becoming through their learning, notices who they have already become, helps them dream optimistic dreams, and celebrates their victories, large and small.

John Gottman, a psychologist who studies couples, discovered that a couple that has four or five positive interactions for every negative interaction they have is far more likely to stay together than couples who only have three positive interactions for every negative interaction. The positive interactions insulate the couple from the damage caused by the negative interactions.

Similarly, the relationship between parents and children suffers if the positive interactions drop below that 4:1 ratio. Moreover, parents are often the only people who have the opportunity and skills to make up for negative experiences children have with teachers and other children. An increasing number of schools are encouraging teachers to maintain a 4:1 positive to negative interaction ratio with students, which is an excellent trend. However, parents have an easier time learning what each individual child will consider positive and negative simply because teachers are working with more children at a time and different children each year.

If your child has a teacher who maintains a 2:1 positive to negative ratio with your child, then your child comes home from school with a positivity deficit. A positivity deficit puts a child under stress and triggers flight, fight, freeze responses through the release of adrenaline and cortisol. A child with a positivity deficit reacts to life as though they are constantly under threat.

Under threat, children suffer the same physical and cognitive challenges that adults deal with when threatened, but with fewer resources. How do you feel when you are unrecognized at work and you think the boss doesn't like you? What tools do you have to work with? When your child goes to school and gets mediocre marks and has friendship challenges on the playground, they are that stressed and also have not learned the tools to manage the stress.

The tools of Inspiration are designed to reduce the threat assessment level to the point that the child has access to their full, creative resourcefulness.

Acknowledge

Acknowledgement is stating out loud what is currently wonderful about the person your child is. Notice that this is really focused on qualities of the child and not things the child has done.

If we praise our children for their accomplishments, we run the risk of making them feel that unless they accomplish lots of things, they are not worthy of our love and recognition. This can be a disaster if they find themselves in a situation where they are overwhelmed, blocked from accomplishing things, or otherwise do not feel successful enough. They may be ashamed to come and share their struggles with us just when they need our support the most.

When we acknowledge our children for the qualities we see in them, they come to see themselves that way. Human beings are notoriously bad at understanding themselves. We are often blind to what other people see clearly. We cannot count on our children to see the good things about themselves that we see in them. They need us to tell them the good things about themselves.

A powerful acknowledgement does not include any commentary or qualification. In particular, it should not to be tied to an accomplishment or to imply that they sometimes are or "can be" that way. We want them to believe that we see that quality in them even when they are having a bad day and it isn't on display. A nice side effect of this practice is that over time it becomes easier for us to see and remember that their good qualities are always part of who they are.

To acknowledge your child, say, "You are..." and simply name the quality. You are brave. You are kind. You are thoughtful. You are persistent. You are strong.

In the Appendix is a list of qualities to start you thinking. Come up with your own list. What kind of person do you want your child to be? Add those.

Validate

To validate something is to demonstrate that it is true or valuable. We all need to be validated. We need to have our value reflected back to us by others. We need to have others accept that our experience is true for us. We need to know that we aren't crazy. Validating our children means accepting their understandings of their experience.

Have you heard a parent say to a child, "Stop crying. It isn't that bad?" To the child, whatever happened was bad enough that it made them cry. To suggest otherwise is to invalidate the child's feelings. Think about how you feel when you are upset that a friend is late for the 157th time and they say, "It's just five minutes. It's not like it's a big deal," when you see punctuality as a sign of respect, and it feels like a very big deal indeed to you.

Validation takes many forms.

"I can see that you are really upset. That must have meant a lot to you."

"You are crying. I bet it feels like a really big deal."

"Wow. You really did that!"

You do not have to agree with something to validate it. You can think something is really not a big deal in the grand scheme of things and still honestly say, "This seems to be really important to you."

Be careful not to validate in the first half of a sentence what you invalidate with the second half. "This seems to be really important to you, but in the grand scheme of things it isn't," makes them wrong for having such strong feelings. Much better to say, "This seems to be really important to you, and to me it seems like maybe it's not such a big deal in the grand scheme of things." See how this sentence validates both the child's experience and the parent's perspective. Both things can be true at the same time.

Validation in this form is a way of respecting the child. Children do not have much perspective. They have so little experience in and of the world that each new thing feels much more important than the same thing will in a few years. It is tempting to think we should be teaching them how the world really works at all times. But we don't need to.

Children are naturally creative, resourceful, and whole. They are going to learn about the world by living, one experience at a time. We will be more effective at helping them learn if we focus on making sure that their learning faculties, their pre-frontal cortexes, are operating at full capacity.

Anything that triggers the body to produce cortisol decreases their prefrontal cortex processing. That's a feature, not a bug. When our children are under a real threat to their survival, we want that flight/fight/freeze response to take full control and get our children out of danger as fast as possible without them pausing to overthink things.

When we take a child to the emergency room after an accident and the nurse asks the child how much it hurts, the nurse knows that the child may not be able to report accurately. The top end of the scale is "the most pain you can imagine." Children may not be able to imagine as much pain as it is possible to experience. But the scale validates the child's experience of pain by making sure there is no way the child can be wrong. On the scale of "not at all" to "as much as you can imagine," whatever the child says is right. And, of course, it is only one data point. The nurse measures the child's vital signs and looks at the injury before deciding what triage level is appropriate.

Parents can do the same. We validate the child's experience to help the child feel that they matter. We use the wider context to help us decide how to respond.

Identify Values

Most people crave the experience of feeling that they are fully alive and expressing who they are. For adults, this involves setting goals that align with our values and tuning our minds and skillsets to most effectively get us there.

For children, the process has the same elements but is often less cognitive. With young children, what feels good and what is fun tend to be the driving values. Slowly, over time, these categories become more complex. We learn to distinguish between things that feel good now but are temporary, things that feel good now but make things feel worse later, things that feel good now and continue to feel good later, and things that feel bad now but lead to really good things. Each of these lessons can only be learned through experience.

Coaches help their clients identify the values that drive their lives by listening to the stories they tell, observing the choices they make, and noticing what they avoid. Parents help their kids discover their values in much the same way.

Look for patterns. Does your child consistently hurry to finish first or do they take their time? Do they take their time on school work and rush through dessert or vice versa? Do they gravitate to nature or architecture, pets or wild animals, stories or problems, groups or individual activities? These preferences are where values form.

Children often need to try many things to discover

what they like. Encouraging wide exploration rather than early specialization helps a child who isn't sure develop a choice of options. A child who specializes too early may later regret not having been exposed to a wider array of possibilities. It is worth keeping some variety even for a child who seems to only have one passion.

Children are born ready to learn through following the impulse to have fun. Through learning, they develop their own sense of values. To feel their own sense of fulfillment as adults, they will need to find ways of living that are mostly in line with these values. But until they have identified their values, they cannot develop goals and dreams that are in line with such values.

Some values are inherent in our genetic makeup as they are part of basic human drives. These include autonomy, connection, and competence. You can assume your children have these values while they are discovering what else matters to them.

Parents and schools often try to impose values on children or tell them what their goals should be. This is not a coaching approach.

The coaching approach is to help the child discover their own values and to support them in their efforts to build lives that fit those values. This can be very difficult when a child develops values that are in some conflict with the values that their parents hold most important. This is a place where parental self-management is very important for maintaining a supportive and loving connection between parent and child.

Children and parents often differ in their values. Sometimes significantly. Validating the values of the child and supporting them when the child knows that it is a stretch or challenges your values is an incontrovertible signal to the child that you see them for who they are and that you love them. To love someone enough that you will help them achieve goals that you would not choose if you could make the choice is extremely powerful. Obviously, there are some values that are so against your values that to support a child to violate them is more than you can do, but simply validating their goals and being transparent about how challenging it is to love someone who has different values goes a long way to helping them navigate the world.

An unfortunate, or at least complicating, truth about human beings is that we are not internally consistent. Sometimes our values conflict with each other and we have to prioritize one over another.

In addition, sometimes we realize that the things we say we value are the things we think we should value whereas the choices we make about our lives reflect that we actually prioritize other things. Sometimes we choose not to live in ways that honor our values because we are afraid of the consequences or we lack required skills. Before we can change our actions, we must identify the values that we really want to live by and accept where we fall short or are forced to compromise.

We can teach our children that inconsistency and imperfection are part of the human condition and that they are manageable. We can model responding to this reality with acceptance and self-compassion rather than shame and self-judgment.

Injecting Positivity

Sometimes countering the negativity bias is best done by deciding to do anything that creates positive experiences. Pure fun. Dance parties. Going to a playground. Telling bad jokes. Telling good jokes. Life shouldn't all be about work.

Sometimes a laugh during a tough conversation is exactly what is needed to break through the heat and remind people what is important.

Remember that when the brain and body feel under

threat, learning is severely diminished. There is no teachable moment when stress is that high. There is nothing wrong with abandoning a challenging conversation and talking about the latest thing your kid is fascinated by if it lightens the mood enough for them to be open to being coached.

All the different techniques that are part of Inspiration are different ways of injecting positivity. They have value that also provides long term learning and growth as a byproduct. But at their heart, they are forms of injecting positivity. While you are learning the tools, slowly over time, it is useful to keep in mind the general principle.

If all you remember from this section is that you inspire through injecting positivity, you will have a powerful tool. You might even reread this book in a year and realize that you invented variations of acknowledgement and validation and that you have been helping your children identify their values.

These things aren't complicated to understand. They take practice to make habitual. For many people, they also go against some of the ways they were raised and taught. They are not the approaches of all your family, friends, and nosey neighbors who feel better about themselves after they have criticized your parenting. But if you understand why you want to do them and how they lead to what is important to you, you will find your own motivation to continue practicing.

When we move from Inspire to Facilitate, we shift to skills that are part of all approaches to trying to reach goals, but how we do them from a coaching perspective may feel strange and unfamiliar.

As you read the next section, take your time. Remember that if you have adopted the four foundational principles and are listening to learn and acting to inspire your children, you will have activated their creativity and resourcefulness. You don't have to do all the work.

STAGE THREE: FACILITATE

Coaches facilitate learning and growth. Benefiting from that facilitation is the primary reason people hire coaches. The fun part about being a coach is that it doesn't matter what challenge a client is facing, coaching always uses the same skills. Many coaches are best at helping clients solve problems the coach has never faced. Subject matter expertise can actually get in the way of good coaching. Once you adopt a coach approach to parenting, you can stop feeling bad about not knowing everything about everything your child might need to learn. Your not-knowing can be a gift to your children.

Parents who embrace a coach approach will find that they are relieved of the burden of some of their teaching roles. Most of the skills we want children to have are skills they will need eventually. If we wait until they have already determined a need for the skill, they will have their own internal motivation to learn and we can simply facilitate that learning. This is much easier to do than to try to teach children skills they do not want to learn.

Figuring out what knowledge kids want to acquire and helping them learn makes parenting easier. Much of what children are expected to learn at various ages is determined by how schools are structured and what experts say children should be capable of at any given age.

If we focus on what we think children should be capable of doing at any given age, we are molding them into our vision of a good child. This is counter to the coaching perspective or helping the child that is here now grow into the adult that they want to become.

It is a radical mindset shift for some. If you are struggling with it, take your time to process it.

When we mold children into what we want, we are teaching them to conform, to adapt, to yield to external force. Many children do this willingly for beloved parents and teachers. And it does not always serve them well as adults.

In my coaching work with adults, I am fundamentally helping them become leaders of their own lives. I support them as they stop making everybody else happy and focus on becoming the person that they want to be. Invariably, a significant part of what they want is love, connection, and belonging and this desire, combined with clear expectations of who they had to become in order to make their parents happy, has led them to become people pleasers who resent the sacrifices they make for others. They don't want to stop being kind, respectful, responsible, and generous or successful at work. They want to honor both needs in ways that respect their full humanity. If they had been taught how to do this as children, they would still be successful adults and I would be out of work.

This stage of the L.I.F.T. framework has more tools and specific skills than the previous sections. I have included more examples and specific things to try. These are skills that can be learned, and practice will make you more comfortable and effective.

Facilitation has three elements: setting goals, implementation, and reassessing. The section on reassessing presents the coach approach to discipline.

Goal Setting

Helping kids decide what they really want to do is not always easy and is often a cyclical process. But then again, this is true for adults as well. Figuring out how often to revisit goals is more of an art than a science. It does help to schedule it so that it becomes part of your routine as well as spontaneously jumping in when you sense the need.

Adults often work on a 30-, 60-, or 90-day cycle with quarterly or annual reviews. With children, the beginning of each school term and the beginning of summer are natural reassessment points. A family might want to create its own timing based on family traditions. In my house for instance, we reflect on goals heavily at the beginning of any academic period that includes new classes (September for the elementary school kids, September and February for the high schooler) and lightly at the beginning of a new sports season and on the equinoxes and solstices.

Setting a new habit that occurs infrequently is more challenging than setting a daily habit. There are too few repetitions for it to become familiar and comfortable quickly. It is worthwhile to keep at it. You have plenty of time to create annual rituals with your children that become comfortable routines.

What are your long-term goals for your children? You probably want them to be happy and successful. You probably also have some ideas about what they need to have in their lives in order to be happy and successful. Some of these ideas are intangible. You want them to be kind, respectful, loved, loving, and the like. Others are more tangible. You want them to have a good job. You may think they will be happiest if they get married and have children. You may think home ownership is a path to happiness or a path to frustration. You may think the career you chose was one people should avoid at all costs.

What about short-term goals? You want them to do well on tomorrow's spelling test, play well in next weekend's basketball game, and be respectful towards the family friend who is coming to visit next week while in the middle of a difficult divorce.

But these aren't the kinds of goals that are easily measurable. How will you know whether you are successful in helping your children reach them?

If you can't set useful goals for yourself, how can you help your children set goals? Short answer, you can't. For the purposes of explaining how to set goals, I am going to start with talking about setting good goals in general. Then, I will discuss how this model might work with children's goals as they change over time.

Goals are domain specific, which means that you will have social goals, economic goals, health goals, etc. and they will not necessarily be the same. Personal success coach Brian Tracy suggests that adults should have 3-5 professional goals, 3-5 personal goals, and 3-5 health and wellness goals each year. Adults can generally handle that many goals when they are domain specific. More than 3-5 goals in any area is too many for adults. Children often do better with 1-3 goals at a time and can handle different goals at school, at home, and in an extra-curricular activity.

It is easy to drive yourself or your child to burnout by having too many goals and working too hard to meet them. Patience is a virtue. Many of the things we most want our children to learn are things we are still perfecting in ourselves. The most important tasks of life are life-long learning processes. Start where you are and take the next step. Remember to build from what exists right now. If you try to hurry the process, things will crumble. If things already feel overwhelming, just pick one good goal and work toward that.

What makes a good goal?

Good goals have an aspirational element that motivate us and a measurable element that allow us to assess whether or not we are making progress. When a goal has both of these elements, we can see how the tasks we are working on build towards the things we really care about even when the tasks themselves are frustrating or boring.

Kids are often asked to do tasks without having a reason to do them other than obedience to teachers and parents. If we help our children identify their aspirations, we can help them connect the tasks with the big picture. It isn't always easy.

Like many parents these days, I have a son who wants to be a video game designer, a highly competitive field that requires lots of luck and years of development to get into. The more I can help him connect the subjects he doesn't like or find easy in school with that goal, the easier it is for him to find the motivation to keep working. Some of the connections are tenuous and he needs to be reminded of them frequently. This is normal.

Many kids do not have specific visions for what they want to do when they grow up. This often makes adults uneasy because it is hard to help children plan for a future that is not well defined. But it is not impossible.

We know from Martin Seligman's work in the field of positive psychology that human flourishing requires five elements: positive emotions, a sense of engagement or agency, good relationships, a sense of meaning or purpose (awareness that we matter), and achievement. He uses the acronym PERMA to remember that.

For kids, I prefer GAMER.

G is for good feelings.
A is for accomplishments.
M is for make a difference.
E is for effective.
R is for relationships.

If we teach our kids that these five elements are important for everybody, they can explore how they might create more of each of them in their lives during the next school year. One year at a time, they will learn more about what helps them experience those elements and this knowledge will help them set better goals in the future.

As a culture, we have adopted some misunderstandings about passion and purpose. These myths make it harder than it has to be for us to help our kids create a life filled with good feelings and a sense that they matter. "Follow your bliss," and "Do what you love, and the money will follow," make it sound like bliss and love exist in the beginning, but that is not how passion and bliss work. Passion and bliss are discovered and developed. We come to value what we put effort into.

A marriage might start with a spark of attraction and infatuation, but to become a mature love relationship, it must work its way through hard interpersonal struggle to a skilled and negotiated co-existence between two completely different approaches to life. Similarly, a career might start with a spark of attraction, but without hard work learning the craftmanship required to do it well, it will never develop into a true passion.

Goal setting can help our kids get over the hurdles between initial excitement and deep commitment. It is a several part process.

1. Set the aspirational goal.
2. Decide on 1-3 measurable goals that are required in order to meet the aspirational goal or that would be evidence that you are moving in the right direction, toward the aspirational goal.
3. Track progress towards the measurable goals and develop practices for getting going again when things have stalled.
4. When the measurable goals are 80% complete, reassess and set new goals.

It is important not to insist on perfection before checking to make sure that aspirations haven't changed. It often turns out the perfection is not required or that perfection is not possible given circumstances that are out of your control. It is important to celebrate 70-80% complete as substantial progress. Remember that the actual goal is the aspirational goal. The measurable elements were expected signposts on the way, as predicted with incomplete information.

If we were driving to a cottage for a vacation and were told to make a left at the corner with the McDonald's, we would not keep driving on the road if we noticed that the place the McDonald's used to be now has a Burger King. We would make that left turn anyway because what we really want is to get to the cottage.

It can be harder to make that left anyway if the real goal isn't tangible and we aren't exactly sure what tangible elements will be required to create it. Nevertheless, we must learn to make that left turn. How many adults have you heard say, "I should have left that situation years ago, but I wasn't sure where else to go?" We need to reassess periodically to make sure we are still heading in the direction that we want to go.

Children need to reassess far more frequently than adults because they are starting with less information. There is no easy way to learn the things they need to learn. The learning is in the wrong paths, the misdirections, and the mistakes. If children have a single-minded goal like that of my son who is convinced that being a video game designer is the only path that will lead to positive emotions, I should be working to facilitate his confirmation of the rightness of that goal by helping him hit measurable goals that include testing whether it really is a good path for him to commit himself to.

Aspirational goals should be inspirational, a stretch, and able to be met in many different ways. Measurable goals need to be specific, achievable, quantifiable, testable, and time-dependent. A complete goal includes both elements.

For example: I want to be a great videogame designer,

so by next month I will have registered for the next class offered by the local computer club, storyboarded two new scenes in the game I am designing, and gotten my younger brother to give me feedback on one scene he hasn't seen yet.

Implementing

Once goals have been set, the next task is to help your children progress towards those goals. This is not always easy. Most of us have to learn how to help our kids get out of their own way without inadvertently putting extra obstacles in their way ourselves.

Most of us have stories we can tell of times that our parents, teachers, or supervisors said things to us that paralyzed us or otherwise derailed us despite them having our best interests in mind and wanting us to succeed.

I will never forget the short descriptive piece I wrote in middle school in which I was trying to create a soft, still mood that evoked the hush of a breezeless, foggy morning by the ocean when the water was calm, the silence was thick and heavy, and the whole world seemed to have paused. I wrote the piece in the passive voice because I thought that would convey the sensation of suspended animation I was trying to achieve. When I got the paper back from my instructor, the only marks on the page were a red circle around every verb and the comment "Use active voice." I stopped trying to create moods through description for decades after that feedback.

A coachlike response to that piece would have assumed that I was naturally creative and resourceful and invoked curiosity. My teacher could have said, "Kate, you don't usually use the passive voice this much and you used it all the time here. What's up with that?" I would have been able to tell her about my desires for the piece and she would have had an opportunity to help me find some still verbs that I could use in the active voice. The fog could have rested on the water. The water could have nestled in the cove. The birds could have suspended their activities. She could have facilitated my development as a writer. Instead, I felt shamed and attacked for having tried something experimental and decided there was no point in trying to do anything interesting. More to the point, I still didn't understand why it would be more effective to avoid the passive voice.

In fact, I learned the lesson she tried to teach me years later when I fell in love with a book that had large sections in the passive voice. The author had used the passive voice for all the sections of a novel that happened in a city where time didn't pass. The first time I read the book, the effect worked. Those sections of the book did read like time had stood still, especially in contrast to the activity in the rest of the book. But on rereading, those sections were dead and lifeless and hard to stomach. I started skipping those sections. I knew that nothing happened except a growing sense of frustration within the character who would eventually break the magic and release time. I was bored. In the other sections of the book, despite knowing what was coming, I continued to be engaged and never skipped a page. The third time I reread that book, I knew the danger of writing in the passive voice and the lesson didn't come with the side order of shame that my teacher had inadvertently dished up when she was trying to help me.

As parents, we are going to make mistakes and we have to learn to live with that. At the same time, we can work to make such unintended negative consequences of our good intentions as infrequent and minor as possible.

It takes more time to dig into the challenge than it does to assume we know what's right and necessary for learning. The good news is that investing the time early often results in our kids taking responsibility for themselves earlier than they would otherwise. In the long run, we have to do less for them. It is counterintuitive, but slowing down right now often speeds up the overall process.

The following tools help us use a slow moment as a catalyst: asking powerful questions, vanquishing inner demons, changing perspective, increasing awareness, and nudging forward or deeper.

Asking Powerful Questions

For many people the experience of being coached includes profound aha moments in response to great questions. A typical coaching session transcript would frequently look to an untrained eye like a conversation in which the coach does nothing but ask questions. A session that includes a lot of the coach talking has usually turned into teaching or mentoring rather than coaching.

The turning point in a coaching conversation is often punctuated by the client saying, "That's a really good question," and falling silent for a while.

What makes a really good question? A really good question is a powerful question that is asked at a time that it matches the client's growing edge. Part of the art of coaching is not being attached to any particular question being the right question. Many coaching questions are powerful questions at not quite the right time. The trick is to make sure as many of your questions as possible are powerful and then be patient and keep trying until one matches the readiness of your kid.

Which leads us to the investigation of what makes a question powerful. A powerful question is short, simple, and open-ended. It helps the person who was asked walk down what Chris Argyris and Peter Senge call the ladder of inference to understand and unpack their own unconscious mental processing. This provides new awareness that creates an opening to revise assumptions, interrupt patterns, and change directions.

At the bottom of the ladder is all the data we could possibly observe in the world, all the facts and qualities of existence. The first step up is the data that we actually perceive. Human beings don't see infrared. We are physiologically incapable of even sensing all of the possible data points that exist at any given moment. We always have incomplete data, though in some cases we can use technology to reduce that incompleteness somewhat.

The next step up is the data that our brains consider worth paying attention to. This is where making sure that our children (and ourselves) are functioning from our most creative, resourceful selves is important. When our threat assessment systems have gone to yellow or red, far less information in the world is considered relevant. When we are being chased by a bear, the color of the birds in the nearby trees is absolutely irrelevant. When our kids are in danger of running into traffic, we probably won't hear our phones ring. We cannot learn from data that our brains don't consider relevant enough to let past this first filter. It simply never enters the system.

Once our brains have decided information is relevant, they filter that information through our knowledge and assumptions about how the world works, our judgments about what is important, and our awareness of our own competencies to choose the next course of action and set the processes in motion for us to take that action. If any of this processing is flawed (and it frequently is), the action that results is less than ideal.

Our most deeply embedded mental habits involve running up the ladder from information to action without conscious thought. When our habits are good, speed is great. It improves our efficiency dramatically. When our habits are not so great, speed is a problem. We find ourselves miles down a path in the wrong direction before we even notice we took a wrong turn.

Observing our conscious processing reveals the computation and calculation our brain typically does without our notice. Helping our children learn to observe their conscious processing helps them learn about themselves and learn to question their own convictions.

Children have less experience than adults, so their knowledge about how the world works is more flawed and their assumptions may be more off. Not always though. Adults are often blind to facts children see because most adults have solidified their assumptions about the world in ways that limit the amount of information their brains consider important. People have blind spots. They do not notice that they have filtered out details and are often shocked and dismayed when they are forced to deal with facts that contradict their assumptions.

Our children also struggle with challenges to their assumptions and understandings, which is why validation is important. Validation allows us to acknowledge that given their experience it makes absolute sense for them to see the world the way they do AND we have additional information that means we see it differently.

Facts are at the bottom of the ladder of inference, so the most powerful questions are aimed at bringing more facts to consciousness. Most powerful questions start with "What..." Teenagers and some younger children have the self-awareness to observe their own thinking processes, in which case questions that start with "How..." can be powerful.

Questions that start with "Why..." are rarely effective in creating opportunities for learning and growth. Think about yourself for a moment. When someone asks you why you did something, how often do you feel like you are being asked to justify having done it. Asking why frequently makes people defensive.

More than that, when you ask someone why they did something, they cannot answer the question without either saying "I don't know" or making up an answer even if they don't know. "I don't know" is an incredibly difficult answer for any human being to give to a question. It requires the self-confidence to know that you are a worthy human being even when you are incompetent and ignorant. Most adults struggle with this in at least some areas of life. Asking children to be more mature than adults is a recipe for disaster. Making up an answer feels much safer to the ego.

The trouble with making up an answer is that our brains don't handle the complexity of lying well. When we make something up, our brains assume that we are telling the truth and the thing we made up becomes part of the unconscious information through which all new information is filtered. When we ask our children to explain why they did something, we are helping them build the internal systems that will lead to them doing it again. So we should only ask them why they do things that we know for sure they should keep doing.

One danger with the What/Why distinction that parents need to remember is that "what were you thinking?" is a way of asking "why?" It is not a powerful question.

In addition to helping someone walk down the ladder of inference, a powerful question is short, simple, and open-ended. Remember that part of what makes a question really good is when it matches the respondent's growing edge. Coming up with the answer is a stretch but not so big a stretch that it feels scary. A really good question is slightly off-kilter from the respondent's current thinking but not by so much that it seems irrelevant.

The shorter and simpler the question, the more likely the recipient's brain will interpret it in a way that makes them think. And an open-ended question provokes inquiry rather than stopping discussion. A closed question is either a question that asks for a yes or no answer or one that comes with an implied right answer. Powerful questions are never rhetorical. They always come from genuine curiosity.

Some of the most powerful questions are:

- What is important to you about that?
- What's up with that?

- What's going on there?
- What do you already know?
- What's next?
- What does that mean to you? or What does [word they used] mean to you?
- What else?

Use the language your kids use as much as possible in your questions.

You need to not be attached to how your child answers the question. In their head, they are focused on themselves. They are listening from the first type of listening. And this is what you want when you are coaching them. Paying attention to themselves is how they learn about themselves and help themselves grow. You do not know how they are thinking in this moment. You have to trust that they are resourceful and creative and are interpreting the question in a way that their naturally developing and learning brain thinks will help them get towards their goals.

You need to be ready to build from whatever your child gives you as an answer. You cannot predict their response. You need to trust that you are creative and resourceful and will figure out what step is a good next step once you hear the answer your child gives you. Practicing the voice mirroring exercise discussed in the section on listening is useful for gaining that confidence.

Vanquishing Inner Demons

As adults, we have inner voices of self-sabotage that tell us we aren't good enough, we aren't worthy, and we aren't loveable. If we have reasonable self-awareness, we know that we are more than these voices. Often, in fact, we can hear these phrases in our minds as if spoken by people from our past. Some of those negative thoughts become part of our self-identity, though, and we have to work hard to separate our sense of self from the negative messages.

Coaches working with adults help them separate their self-identity from these negative thoughts.

These inner demons take our fears and doubts and turn them into good reasons why we can't build the life we want. We must learn to vanquish them in order to make progress towards creating a life that feels fulfilling.

Children develop the same doubts and have the same need to vanquish these demons. However, due to their inexperience, they have few resources to bring to the fight. Parents have an opportunity to help their children keep a sense of separation between themselves and their doubts, preventing the negative voices from solidifying into a sense of identity.

In the early stages of development, children do not have any sense of separation from their emotional experiences. Things that feel good draw them near and things that feel bad drive them away. Slowly, unconscious pattern recognition grows and levels of abstract understanding develop. Only then do cognitive thoughts about experience have a chance to develop.

Parents can help this cognitive awareness develop by telling their children what they see. "You were angry and you hit me. When you felt like hitting me, that was the angry part of you telling you to hit me. You don't have to do what the angry part of you says. You can choose. You made an unwise choice because you hurt me. Now, I am angry and don' want to do anything nice for you until you find a way to make me feel better. "

The parent takes a stand on behalf of the wise part of the child. The one that wants to find positive ways to get love, connection, and belonging. The parent trusts that if the child believes strongly enough that part of them that can act without listening to the angry part of them it will become true. The parent models a way of thinking that increases the separation between the different inner impulses.

There are many stories in many traditions of a good

voice whispering in one ear and a bad voice whispering in the other ear and the need to pay attention to the good voice rather than the bad voice. The good voice is the voice of love, optimism, and compassion. The bad voice is the voice of fear, contempt, and hatred. These two voices represent consciousness dominated by the pre-frontal cortex and conscious experience through the fear response. As a basic metaphor, they are a reasonable place to start. But the good/bad distinction is overly simple.

A more nuanced approach is to see them both as allies. The voice of fear is not bad per se. Fear is a warning that attention must be paid. But fear has a hard time telling a real danger from an apparent danger. A motion sensor outside a house could be triggered by robbers or a raccoon. Similarly, a child's threat assessment warning could go off when they are about to lose a board game or when they nearly drop a treasured toy in a lake.

A coach approach to fear is to investigate what the fear is pointing at. What should attention be paid to? What is the concern underlying the fear?

The younger and less verbal the child, the more you will need to guess what is going on. As they get older, they will be able to tell you more.

Kids may not think of worry as a fear response. They may think of fear as being big–like being afraid of snakes and running away. You might ask, "What bad thing is your brain trying to prevent?"

Building a friendly relationship with fear can be as simple as getting in the habit of thanking fear for pointing out something we should pay attention to.

It can be useful to think of fear as an inner younger sibling. It has good instincts but hasn't learned much yet, so it needs the wise part of the child to actually decide whether it's a real threat and if so what to do about it.

Let your kids know that the different parts of themselves are like a cohort of supervillains. Each villain has a different fear that they bring to the surface. Each villain prompts a different kind of bad choice. Luckily, the kids also have a cohort of inner superheroes who work together like the Avengers or the Justice League to fight off their inner supervillains.

Have them think of a recent example of a poor choice. What specific behavior did they engage in? Why did an inner supervillain want that behavior? What goal that is important to your child was the villain trying to accomplish? Remember that the inner supervillain thought they were helping your child even though they went about it in a problematic way.

Every supervillain has a weakness. Can your kids identify the weaknesses in their inner supervillains and create superpowers or gadgets that their inner superheroes can use to exploit those weaknesses?

Changing Perspective

Our perspective is how we see the world. The unconscious part of our perspective comes from the parts of the ladder of inference that we run up without noticing. For younger kids, their whole perspective is unconscious. We can help shape their perspective implicitly and explicitly. The younger they are the more implicit we have to be. The sooner we can start making it explicit, however, the sooner they will start doing this work for themselves. This is yet another opportunity to slow down to speed up and to relieve pressure on ourselves.

Change is always stressful. Changing our perspectives can be especially challenging because our perspective is part of our sense of identity. Our egos don't like it. As adults, we can use rational explanations to combat the fear, but creative and playful ways of creating such change go over more easily. Children need time to develop the rational faculties and body of experience that allow them to go directly at the work of changing perspectives. It is useful to have fun and playful ways of helping them

Stories and metaphors are the most powerful tools in your arsenal. Kids are story-telling beings. All humans are, but kids even more than adults. The reason so many lessons for children are embedded into fables, fairy tales, myths, and stories is because this is how children learn without fear. They discover useful patterns of behavior and not so useful patterns of behavior through witnessing characters try various approaches to problem-solving in stories. The characters become a way for them to connect with the experience.

Our brains can't tell the difference between fiction and non-fiction in some interesting ways. When we imaginatively connect to a character's experience, we learn as if we had also lived through that experience. The younger we are, the more stories feel real and the more powerful the impact of this imaginative learning.

The stories children hear and the stories about the world they write in their own heads become the understandings of the world and assumptions they use to filter information as they run up the ladder of inference. When you hear people talk about changing your story to change your life, this is what they are talking about. When we change the stories that color how we interact with the world, the calculations and computations our unconscious mind performs come up with different answers and everything about how we engage with the world changes.

One of the things we can help our children with is finding and writing inner stories about their world that help them achieve their goals.

The danger in actively trying to change our children's perspective through stories is that they can see right through us. We should not give our children stories with the intention of teaching them the message in the story. This will teach them that there is a right way to read a story and that our gifts of so-called entertainment come with an agenda and are about our needs and not their desires. We have to be careful to be unattached to the lessons our children take from stories. They are making up stories based on what they experience in the world faster than they learn from books.

And yet, stories, fables, and fairy tales throughout history have been used to convey truths about the world. Trust that your children are naturally creative and resourceful and will unfold and develop in their own time. Tell them a variety of stories that are entertaining, silly, scary, and captivating. When they are ready to learn a lesson, you will have given them all the material they need to learn it. You can nudge them by selecting stories that have morals you want them to learn close to the surface.

One of my kids loved a manners book called *Do Unto Otters: A Book About Manners* by Laurie Keller because of the puns and a silly joke that ran throughout the book. I find it hard to believe that he didn't also pick up some of the messages about how to be a good friend over the many times we read it, but he wasn't ready for all of them and they didn't directly turn into behavioral change. Learning is like that. We plant seeds. They grow or wither in their own time. We just keep planting seeds until one sprouts. And then we nurture that one as much as we can in hopes it grows to bloom. But anyone who has ever overwatered a plant knows that part of gardening is waiting for nature to take its course.

You can use stories and imagination as part of coaching your children. When one of your children is struggling with something that feels hard, you might ask them how a favorite character would handle the problem.

Will they let you pretend to be that character whispering advice in their ear? If so, tell them that you don't know the character as well as they do. Ask, "what advice should I give you as I pretend to be that character?" Then repeat back to them the words they give you when it seems appropriate. If you use the words they give you, you are helping them make a connection between themselves and a character they admire. They can begin to internalize the qualities of the character.

If the character would use a magical or fantasy tool, ask them what real life tools they have that might help them like the imaginary tool helps the character. You might be surprised by what comes up.

Focus on the things you already know your kid likes. Don't worry about whether you understand the details of the reference material. Let your kid lead themselves through the process. You can observe and nudge if you see them going in dangerous directions. Be careful only to steer them away from truly dangerous territories and not from all murky waters. Murky waters often contain the greatest learnings.

Increasing Awareness

Children are naturally creative, resourceful, and whole, and yet they are inexperienced and lacking important information in many cases. Increasing their awareness allows their natural creativity to work with more accurate information so they come up with more practical and effective solutions to their problems.

Their creativity and resourcefulness are going to be spontaneously applied to the problems that are most important to them. Don't be shocked when they surprise you with how they apply additional awareness. It's all part of their process of becoming the adults they want to be.

Children need to develop several different kinds of awareness. They need to become aware of their inner processes, their impact on the world, how the world works, and facts about the world that might not be immediately obvious to them. Parents can help with each of these.

To help children become aware of their inner processes, you have two choices.

First, you can narrate your own inner processes. Many parents do this with preverbal children. After some time, most people get tired of saying everything they think aloud, and they get tired of children saying everything they think out loud. They stop showing their children how they think.

When it comes to things like walking yourself down the ladder of inference to figure out where you got into trouble, however, it can be incredibly powerful to do it aloud in the presence of your children. Doing this validates the kids' experiences of getting into trouble by mistake, shows them that when we make a mistake it is our job to clean up whatever mess was made, and gives them a process they can use to do so. Your life becomes a story they can imagine themselves into enough to start making connections with their own inner experience.

Second, you can use powerful questions to help them investigate their own experience. Good questions include:

- What seemed most important then?
- What did you think [the other person] was thinking? What did you see or hear that made you think that?
- What was your first clue about that?
- What did you notice first?
- What changed your mind?

One of the most powerful tools you can use to help children become aware of their impact on the world is to simply narrate for them your observations of their impact. When they do something and it causes something else to happen, positive or negative, mention it. Do your best to refrain from making any commentary or sharing any judgment. State the facts and let them make their own conclusions. At first, their conclusions may not be what you expect. They may be wildly off. Don't worry.

With time and more experience, they will refine their understanding and get closer to wisdom. Trust that they are learning machines. And they want to learn.

It is especially useful to take time to notice the positive impact of behaviors you want to encourage. When a child seeks relationship through bad behavior, what they are really seeking is the knowledge that what they do impacts the world and that the choices they make matter. When you point out how they are impacting the world around them, they gather evidence that they matter. Knowing that they matter is a fundamental part of what they need to flourish.

You can nudge them towards pro-social behavior by showing the positive impacts that their good choices have. Remember the 4:1 ratio. Fill them up with knowledge that their good choices make the world a place that they want to belong and they are likely to keep making those choices.

Nudging Forward or Deeper

Nudging describes two distinct and powerful tools for parents. In their book *Nudge: Improving Decisions About Health, Wealth, and Happiness*, Richard H. Thaler and Cass R. Sunstein argue that how we structure systems can have a huge impact on what decisions people make. For example, we can make it more likely that our kids will eat healthy food if we don't keep unhealthy snacks in the house.

Nudging in this sense isn't about telling people what they can or cannot do but is about setting up patterns that make it easier to make good decisions. Many parents set their home network Wi-Fi to turn off automatically at a certain time so their kids' (and their own) devices don't connect to the internet. Some people put their alarm clock somewhere they can't reach from lying in bed to get them up without hitting snooze button. These systemic nudges help calm analysis paralysis, moderate decision overwhelm, and reduce tendencies to pick the easy solution over the good solution. They also create comfort with the favored choices because these choices become familiar experiences.

What this form of nudging doesn't do is help children learn how to make their own choices when the options are not so limited, which is the situation in most of the world they will encounter outside your house. The other form of nudging is designed to bridge that gap.

Here, the idea is to keep in mind that every moment could be a learning moment. But, your kids will hate you if you make every moment a learning moment, and you will get sick of working that hard if you try to make every moment a teaching moment. You need to decide when and how much to nudge. The opportunity is always there.

Nudging in this sense is the art of gently pushing the child slowly enough that it doesn't create paralyzing fear. Nudging can either come in the form of getting more depth of understanding around something they already know or about learning something new. It isn't always clear which is which, but the label you give to any piece of learning is less important than having the awareness that you have options, and both are valuable.

Nudging can be done using explicit teaching, acknowledgment, and powerful questions or through active listening and reflecting back what you hear in the wider context of what you are hearing your child say.

In the realm of explicit teaching, we have to remember to keep nudges tiny. What feels small to us may feel overwhelming to a child. We do not know how close to tapped out our children are at any moment and, if possible, we want to avoid pushing them over the top. Their bodies and brains are doing a great job of protecting them and ensuring their survival. If we give them an acknowledgment or ask them a question, they will take in and work with as much as they can at that moment.

When caretaking adults and parents trust that children are creative, resourceful, and whole and that they will develop in their own time, things progress naturally. And if we listen carefully to what isn't being said, we will notice when our children are in need of comfort, soothing, and an injection of positivity rather than learning nudges.

Reassessing

Despite our best intentions and our efforts at helping, sometimes our children will not achieve their goals. When that happens, we must practice the discipline of reassessment.

In most traditional parenting approaches, discipline is the language we use for how we keep kids doing what they are supposed to. In corporate settings, we talk about accountability. These are the same ideas. The common concern is how to help someone be responsible for meeting their goals.

In coaching with adults, the goal is for the coach to hold the client accountable as long as the client needs and then to turn the responsibility for accountability over to the client. This is a form of scaffolding, just like a parent reminding a child to brush their teeth every night until such time as the child starts reminding themselves.

The *Merriam-Webster Dictionary* defines the noun discipline as:

1 a: control gained by enforcing obedience or order
  b: orderly or prescribed conduct or pattern of behavior
  c: self-control
2: punishment
3: training that corrects, molds, or perfects the mental faculties or moral character

The verb form is defined as:

1: to punish or penalize for the sake of enforcing obedience and perfecting moral character
2: to train or develop by instruction and exercise especially in self-control
3 a: to bring (a group) under control

b: to impose order upon

Control, order, punishment, self-control, and training are all possible meanings of the word. A coach approach to parenting does not use punishment to deal with missed goals or failure to do what was agreed. Punishment spoils the relationship between parents and children by introducing unnecessary fear. In *The Prince*, Machiavelli famously wrote, "Better to be feared than loved, if you cannot be both." Notice that the ideal is to be both. If you are loved without any fear of losing you in the background, it is easy for someone to disregard you and treat you poorly. But, if they fear that treating you badly will cause them to lose what they get from you, they have their own internal motivation to be kind to you.

Children have enormous, innate fear of losing their parents' love. It is their prime survival tactic. It is so primal that many adults at midlife still struggle with disappointing their parents.

Parents wear three different hats: family leaders, homemakers, and nurturers of children. In their roles as family leaders and homemakers, order matters, and I will discuss how to use a coach approach and still maintain order in the chapter on Family Matters. As nurturers, parents' key roles are in training and assisting the development of self-control.

Development of self-control is partially a naturally occurring developmental process and partially teachable and trainable. One of the myths of parenting is that all children develop self-control at the same age. They don't. Schools expect a certain level of self-control of students of each age based on statistical averages. Problems occur when there is a mismatch between the development of the child and the expectations of the school. Parents also have expectations, sometimes from educating themselves as parents, but most often from their memories of their own childhoods or feedback from their children's teachers or coaches.

A coach approach trusts that children have natural motivation to learn self-control and they will develop it in their own time while also positioning parents as catalysts to speed up the process.

All the previously discussed tools can be used to provide the child with material they can use creatively to achieve their goals. The following reassessment and accountability framework serves as a lens through which to explore the current situation and discover what might help the child grow into the person they want to become.

When a child fails to achieve a goal, the basic questions you should be asking are: "What got in the way?", "What did you learn from that?", and "What should we do differently next time?"

The two main reasons goals don't get met that individuals have control over are lack of skills and lack of motivation. Bad luck, lack of information, and unforeseen changes in circumstance require resilience to manage and may actually make it impossible for a goal to be met. It is important that parents recognize these possibilities and do not try to make children responsible for things that are outside their control.

Answering these six questions will help you and your child determine what should be changed to make it easier to succeed next time.

- Are there skills the child doesn't have that are required to do the work?
- Is the child really motivated to do the work?
- Does the child have access to the tools and environment necessary to do the work?
- Do the tools and environment support the child's motivation to do the work?
- Is the social situation supporting the child's ability to do the work?
- Is the social situation supporting the child's

motivation to do the work?

Changing the tools and social situation are forms of nudging that are often more easily done by parents than children in the early years. Once children have learned some self-advocacy skills, it becomes easier for them to take responsibility for some of that work. Figuring out how much they can take on for themselves at any given time requires getting curious about exactly what their skills and motivation levels are at the current moment and building from that.

Once you have identified the obstacles that prevented your child from accomplishing the goal, you can create a plan to remove those obstacles. As always, the child's current level of development is the guide to how much the parents needs to do for the child and how much the child should be expected to do for themselves. Children should be encouraged to do as much for themselves as they can and a touch more. Just like an infant learning to walk does best when the parent compliments them on their persistence, encourages them to keep trying, gives them a hand when they get wobbly, and reminds them when they fall that they are getting better all the time, a child of any age does best when they are gently urged to keep stretching to do something that is just a little outside their skillset at a time when they are internally motivated to do the task.

Any of the tools discussed previously can be used to help increase motivation. For example, a parent may help a child change perspective or vanquish their inner demons.

Note that only one of the six questions identifies skills that a child lacks. Teaching skills is only part of how parents support the growth of their children, and we don't always think to teach them the skills they really need. Sometimes, we expect children to intuitively assimilate information and patterns that elude them. When the reassessment process identifies skills our children need to learn, we can let go of any judgment that they are lazy or that there is something wrong with them and focus on teaching them.

Teach is the next and final stage of the L.I.F.T. framework, and we will look at that in the next chapter.

STAGE FOUR: TEACH

On a youth sports team, the coach is expected to both a) plan the strategic approach of the team based on deep knowledge of the strengths and weaknesses of the players on both this team and the opposing team and b) know how to help the players improve and make that happen. It is the second of these tasks that is relevant to the teaching aspect of parenting.

Long term development of youth athletes typically involves drills that are just a little more difficult than the athletes are solidly capable of–once again, learning that stretches them without overwhelming them. Coaches pay attention to the current skill level of their players and push them to be faster, harder, or more precise.

Often cross-training or weight lifting is used to help athletes develop specific muscles independently of the strength and coordination that is developed practicing skills that are part of the game. And coaches work on motivation, goal setting, and accountability as well.

When it is time to play the game, though, coaches have to let the athletes do the work. The coach can nudge and cheer and remind players of things, but too much coaching distracts the players from actually being present in the game. Too much watering makes the plants die. Too much teaching gets in the way of performing.

Parents need to practice the fine art of letting go as well as the craft of designing skill drills.

Drills for Skills They Need

Parent-coaches observe their children and determine what skills are needed and devise ways to build those skills.

Skill drills can come in many forms: extra math worksheets, logic puzzles, discussions over dinner, races against siblings to complete a task, challenges against a timer, games that the kids don't know are developing skills, or minimal supervision of a task while being there as a resource if the kid gets into trouble.

A sports coach has the advantage of getting commitment upfront from players that they will come to practices and do the drills. Parents have to find ways to get their kids to do the work. This typically requires tapping into their internal motivations.

You know your kids. Use what works for them.

As much as possible, avoid implying that they need to do something to make you happy, that knowing more than they do somehow makes you better or more important than them, or that doing this for you will get them a reward. You want to tap into their inner reasons for practicing and improving.

Turn Responsibility Over to Them ASAP

What makes a coaching approach different from many other forms of teaching is that the goal is to turn responsibility over to the students as soon as possible. Better to err on the side of a little too much responsibility plus a compassionate conversation about what to learn from failure than to hold the student's hand for too long.

This is possible because of the twin foundations of trusting the natural creativity and resourcefulness of the child and trusting that growth and transformation will occur in their own time. A coach-parent models for their children that there is no right time table and there is nothing to worry about. The child is where the child is, and the level of development is fine. Resiliency is built on this foundation of trust that the child can and will adapt to anything that happens.

In order to make it safe for the child to fail in this way, the parent must be filling the positivity well, acknowledging the child's good qualities, catching them being skillful, validating their experience, and helping them vanquish their inner demons. The 4:1 positivity ratio discussed earlier is crucial for maintaining motivation and cultivating resilience in the face of learning through failure.

Turning responsibility over to the children can be in the form of asking them whether they are prepared to take on a task or not. If the child says they are not ready, there is an opportunity to explore whether they are not ready because of motivation or a lack of skill or a preference to prioritize something else. Let the child decide.

Older children can be asked how they would like to be supported or if they would like help. When coaching adults, I often ask, "How would you like to hold yourself accountable?" Sometimes they say, "I'm going to ask you to follow up with me next session. Will you do that?" I always say yes. Notice, though, that the act of asking me puts them in the leadership seat. With clients who are less comfortable asking for help, I might say, "How would you like me to keep you accountable?"

With children, it is important to use language that they understand and to respect their current capabilities. Shared responsibility is often appropriate. One approach that honors that children are constantly developing is to ask, "What would you like us to put in place to hold you accountable?" This gives them an opportunity to take responsibility without feeling like you have stopped helping them.

Remember that accountability is not about shame or blame about unmet goals. It is about taking note of where things went wrong and coming up with a plan to stop things going off the rails in the future. You do not need to wait until things have gone off the rails. It is a good idea to reassess periodically, whether things are going well or not.

If the teaching involves imparting information rather than skills, we can ask, "So now that you know that, what do you want to do with it?" or "What seems useful to you about that?" Telling them how to use information or even that they should is taking responsibility away from them and putting the teaching in service of your agenda for them. Coaching supports their agenda for themselves, even when that agenda is vague and still being formed.

Remember, many adults still feel like they don't know what they want to be when they grow up. Expecting children to have vague agendas helps create a sense of ease for everyone.

Intuition

Parents often forget one important tool in their toolbox when they are trying to figure out how to support their children in a particular moment: intuition. As long as the parent maintains their position on the positive side of the fear/love divide, intuition is their friend. Parents who pay attention and listen well at the content and context levels of listening tend to know their children better than they think they do.

Often, a parent cannot articulate why they think something is what their child needs but has a gut feeling. Often this feeling is right. Even when it is not right, it is an interpretation of a relevant piece of data. You can offer your wisdom to your child by saying, "I'm guessing that…", stating your gut feeling, and then asking, "Does that seem like what's going on?"

Always remember that your intuition is processing sensory data through your assumptions and understandings about how the world works, including how people think, and your child (in fact, each of your children if you have more than one) has different assumptions and understandings, possibly very different. To avoid making the child feel unseen or misunderstood, offer your intuition as a gut feeling, a story, a guess, a crackpot theory, or other potentially incorrect idea. Let them confirm or correct it.

Using your intuition well takes a degree of self-management that may not be comfortable to you. Your intuition is a suggestion-making device that is not always correct. You may be used to always either distrusting or believing your gut feelings. If one of these is true for you, practice thinking of your intuitive hunches as best guesses.

The coach approach to parenting decentralizes parental expertise, including intuitive knowing, without rejecting it. This allows parents and children to collaborate despite the power imbalance. This is not the dominant model in our world, though there are a growing number of coaches and psychologists who are teaching this sort of approach and a growing number of schools that look to provide child-led education.

One of the things to be aware of is that mainstream parenting approaches often aren't ideal for any child. They are generally good enough for typical children, and they often become dominant for reasons that have more to do with convenience for the adults in a society than because they are best for kids. The vast majority of kids are highly resilient by nature and have great survival instincts. They learn to adapt to whatever culture they find themselves in and manage moderately well. This is the great genius of humanity as a species.

Some children, however, do not flourish under less than ideal circumstances. Others can only deal with a certain amount of stress before they cannot bounce back. Anxiety and depression are prevalent among teenagers these days. More teens die by suicide than anything other than accidents in Canada and the US and death by suicide is the top killer of teens in the UK. These are warning signs that there are probably better ways to do things. Individual parents are not to blame for these awful statistics. The world is more unsettled than it has been before and is changing faster than the culture is developing new norms of child rearing. What the world needs now is a new approach designed to maximize resilience.

The foundation of resilience is trust that one is naturally creative, resourceful, and whole. Children learn that trust from the trust their parents share with them. When adults create that safety net for their children, children learn that they are capable of handling anything that comes along.

The greatest lessons parents can teach their children is that their agendas matter and they are worthy of the love and support required to pursue them.

In Service of Their Goals

When teaching is offered to children in service of their goals, children believe that they matter. This is one of the fundamental elements of flourishing and one that it is easy for teenagers in particular to feel is missing in their lives. If they have been taught all their lives that they need to follow their parents' agendas and then hit the teenage years, in which their innate developmental agenda is to differentiate from their parents sufficiently to move into independent living, there is a vacuum of time in which they are capable of more than the adult world allows them to do during which gathering evidence that they matter can become an overwhelming challenge.

If we have not already taught teenagers that they matter before they reach this developmental phase, we may not ever get another chance. They may differentiate themselves from us and cease to listen to us just about the time we decide that they are ready to be sent out into the world to fly on their own. Using a coach approach with them when they are younger creates a bond that can withstand the developmental process of differentiation.

It is never too late to start using a coach approach to parenting. Teenagers and young adults who have drifted away from the family are most likely to return if they feel respected and valued as naturally creative, resourceful, and whole even if you disagree with their life choices. It is likely to take some time for them to trust that you really are setting aside your expectations in order to help them flourish, so you will need to be patient and be prepared to be challenged and prove yourself.

If we have the courage to let our children have agendas that are different than our agendas for them would be and make it clear that their agendas for themselves genuinely get priority, we stand a chance of still being an influence in their lives when conventional wisdom says they will no longer be listening to us. And that will be a great reward for the upfront effort invested in doing the self-management required.

When we offer ourselves as parent-coaches in service of our children's goals, we are most likely to achieve our own goals as parents: to raise children who are competent, happy, and connected to their family.

This discussion of the coach approach to teaching as a parent focused on high level strategy and not tactics. This is intentional. The tactics you need will be highly personal. The next chapter, Family Matters, will also be strategic rather than tactical.

To move from strategy to tactics, keep your attention on the strategic goals and chose one action that you think will get you closer to them. After you have taken that action, reassess the situation and chose a next step. You will be able to succeed without having the whole journey planned and you will be able to respond to whatever external forces shake things up.

If you haven't started putting these ideas into practice yet, this is a great time to start. The only way to get better at these skills is to use them. And you will get better with practice. The four stages build on each other in the beginning. Start with Listening to Learn. Then add Inspiring, Facilitating, and Teaching in that order. Once you have introduced Teaching, start experimenting with which stage is the most useful in different situations.

You now have the main L.I.F.T. framework: the four foundations and the four stages. The next chapter will briefly discuss a way to think about your role as the leader of the household that will support you in using a coach approach consistently. After that, we will look at some potential pitfalls.

FAMILY MATTERS

Okay, Kate, I can hear you saying, but what about the fact that I need to get them to school on time, the laundry needs doing, and they won't brush their teeth? I can't just let them run wild. What does your coach approach have to say about that?

So, if you are onboard with the idea of coaching as an approach to helping your kids get the best out of themselves as adults, you need to find a family leadership style that embraces the coach approach without driving you crazy. And that means you have to learn how to lead by enrolling followers rather than by dictation.

Your children did not ask to be part of this family. They are conscripts. Conscripts with a need to keep you happy wired into their very being, but conscripts nevertheless. You have power, rank, and privilege because they need you to ensure their survival.

When they are very young, children want to help. Many parents of older children wistfully remember a time when they could put on music, say it was time to do the clean-up dance, and dance through chores with the children helping beside them. At some point between 12-months and 4 years old, this stops. Children learn that they are separate from their parents and start to assert their authority. From this moment on, there is a power struggle. And much as we hate to admit it, parents do better if we let our egos lose the power struggle at this point. Letting your children know that they are people worthy of respect and catching them doing good are your most powerful enrollment tools. Catching them doing good involves ignoring bad behavior that is not actively unsafe and giving them positive attention when they do the things you want to encourage.

Showing your children that they are people worthy of respect involves listening to them, letting them influence you, taking their positions and interests into consideration when you make decisions that influence them, apologizing when you are wrong, and accepting them for who they are in this moment.

You can be transparent with your kids about the fact that you have a very complicated job as head of the family or as co-leaders of the family. You have to feed, protect, and house the kids, pay the bills, and make sure the housework gets done. When they don't help you around the house, you get cranky and when you get cranky, you stop being fun. You being fun is very important to them.

You want them to make the connection that they have more fun when you like them–not when they obey you, but when you like them. Because when you like them, you give them nice things spontaneously. You like them more when you appreciate how much they are helping.

"Thank you for putting away the laundry. I am so grateful to you. Now I have time for some fun things. I would love to do something fun with you. What would you like us to do together?"

You always love your children, but how often do you like them? It is an important distinction.

It may be faster in the short term to tell kids what to do and to punish them if they disobey. With some kids, that approach backfires even in the short term and their lucky parents are forced to find alternatives. With other kids, you may be able to win the battles, so you have to be careful that you don't lose the war in order to create a sense of order.

You only have so many hours in the day. You need to decide which battles matter to you and which ones don't. The fewer battles you are trying to fight at once, the less stressed you will be and the more you will be able to make the time to slow down and work with your children the way you want to. You do this for you, because you want to be the kind of parent you want to be, not out of obligation and duty. If you do any of this out of a sense of obligation and duty and the sense that you should be this kind of parent, you will resent your children, they will see through you, and you will have lost the war.

It is your job to run the house. The standards you set for tidiness and Pinterest-worthiness are your business. If you are going to insist on things being the way you want them to be, it is your job to either do the work or enroll somebody else to help you. The obvious people to try and enroll are your kids.

Your best motivational tool is your ability to make your children feel loved and safe and valued for who they are. Your second-best tool is your ability to arrange fun activities for them and for you all to do together as a family.

You do not want to train your children to do chores in order to get rewards directly. They will learn that they should be paid for everything they do around the house and this will lead to a lifetime of resenting the fact that running a house is hard work. You want them to learn that helping you feel good makes them feel good. Maybe eventually they will learn to appreciate a clean and orderly house like you do and maybe they won't, but that will be their choice.

You want them to know that when they are nice to other people, other people want to be nice back. So, catch them being good as often as you can and tell them what impact it has on you when they make you feel good. "Thank you so much for doing the dishes without my asking. I really love having the kitchen clean without having to ask you. It makes me feel close to you. And feeling so close to you and having some extra time because I didn't have to ask you to do the dishes means I have some time to do something fun with you. Would you like to play a game with me?" Make sure that what you offer is something you think you will actually enjoy. You want to genuinely like and enjoy the leisure time you spend with your kids. If you don't, you will come to resent them.

Notice that this is not a transaction where they earned the game by doing the dishes. You are training yourself to be generous with them when they do small things that help you out. You are teaching your children that people do nice things for people they feel good about. You are revealing to them a truth about how healthy relationships work. In healthy, loving relationships, people do nice things for each other as gifts and receive nice gestures from the other as gifts. People in healthy relationships do not keep track of exactly how many nice things one person did for the other, but without a reasonable degree of reciprocity, people don't keep giving each other nice gifts.

You are trusting that your children have the universal human desires for love, safety, and belonging and are offering them a possible way to get those. You are helping them craft assumptions and understandings that you hope they will internalize and add to their unconscious processing. You know that small victories repeated turn into habits and habits can be the foundation for next steps in their development. You are teaching them how to be kind and generous people.

Whether they learn from this the lesson that you want is up to them.

Talk with them about the fact that it is your job to help them develop the basic skills they need to be able to live by themselves when they finish school. Tell them what you think those skills are. Ask them to help you. Find out what they want to be able to do for themselves that it might be easier for them to learn from you now while they live in your house. Your job is not to do their job. It is their responsibility to get themselves ready to live on their own. It is your job to be available to show them how if they want help. If you self-manage so that you don't take it personally when they don't do things, then they can decide freely whether to do them or not without feeling like they have to either submit to you or fight you and not do what you say.

Your kids have two conflicting impulses. They want to be competent and capable adults eventually and they want you to take care of them for as long as possible. As they get older, their priorities will change. They will eventually want to learn the things you want them to learn. If you trust that they will develop on their own timetable, you take some of the pressure off them. When they are under less pressure, they will be less likely to erupt into fight/flight/freeze responses.

When they are in creative, resourceful mode, they will be open to learning the things that serve their agendas. You need to practice understanding their agendas sufficiently to see where your agenda and theirs align. It's your job to help them see that.

Delegate as much to them as they are capable of doing. Set goals with them that help them know whether they have achieved them or not. Get curious about what obstacles stop them from meeting those goals. Help them remove those obstacles. Each element of running the house or getting them to school or activities may need to be broken down into very small details at first in order to not overwhelm them as you are training them. Slow down to speed up. They will get there.

You need to get real about the limitations of your capacity and theirs. The modern world is very busy and lots of people are under a huge amount of stress. You need to say no to enough things that you have the time to take care of yourself so you are not running around triggered and overwhelmed. You need to forgive yourself for not being able to do everything.

If keeping up with your neighbors is making you stressed, you need to say no to keeping up appearances. Put your focus on your big goals: you want to raise happy, flourishing adults who want to come home to see their parents for the holidays because they feel loved and accepted for exactly who they are when they do. In comparison, looking good to the folks next door probably doesn't feel so important.

You may decide you want to move to a smaller house so you can hire someone to help out a few hours a week or so you can manage better yourself. You might decide to spend some money on regular help rather than vacations or extra-curricular activities. You might want to pull your kids from some activities. You might decide that letting them spend more time on their devices is a good thing. You might decide that it's time to put away everything that needs dusting until the kids leave home. You have to figure out what works for you.

The world you are raising your family in is not the world that you were raised in. Doing things differently than your parents did doesn't make them wrong. It makes you adaptable.

If you want to have a tight running ship, then you need to be willing to invest the time and energy into enrolling, training, and managing your kids. If you want to use a coach approach to parenting and you don't have that kind of energy, you will need to learn to tolerate some disorder. There is no right answer. There are only answers that work or don't work well enough for your family.

The kids are growing up fast. The more you keep up to date with what they are capable of, the more you will be able to delegate to them.

To run a tight ship, you will be helped by charts,

tracking, regular meetings, individual chats with each kid about how they are doing, clear task assignments, good goals, accountability conversations that look at skills and motivations and similar tools. You get to think of yourself as project manager with a project that will take 18-20 years to complete.

Your goal should be to run a household with an engaged and empowered team of juvenile, unpaid interns. Your goal is to get them involved, empowered, and engaged. You can pull rank here, but you need to make it clear that you are doing it as part of your agenda, not because you think it will make them better people. After all, the whole goal is for them to want to come home for vacations after they have left rather than seeing visiting you as an obligation.

It may sound daunting, but once you implement a coaching-based approach to leading your family, you are likely to discover that you have more fun and an easier time managing your household. If it is new to you, making the transition may feel frightening. You may worry that you are making a huge mistake. The reality is that it is easier that you think. You can do this.

There are just a few ways you might get into trouble and these are discussed in the next chapter. None of them are fatal in small doses and most of them are problems that crop up in every relationship, not just in parenting.

DANGER ZONES

The biggest danger in taking on a coach approach to parenting is in the realm of self-management. When we put ourselves in the service of our kids, we run the risk of forgetting that we have needs of our own. We must take care of ourselves in order to be able to be coachlike with our kids.

We must be willing to stand by while they struggle, knowing that the struggle is part of their learning. This is incredibly difficult for parents. After all, one of our biggest drives is to protect our kids. We must dance on the fine line between letting them learn things the hard way and removing obstacles so they are not overwhelmed and paralyzed by the enormity of their learning tasks.

We must be responsible for our own emotional well-being. We have the same needs as our children. Like them, we must have 1) sufficient positive emotional experiences to balance out the rough times; 2) a sense of agency and self-determination; 3) a sense that we matter and what we do has an impact; 4) good relationships with friends and family; and 5) a sense of accomplishment.

Self-management is required to avoid bringing toxic behaviors into our relationships. Mental and physical health care is required to keep you alive. And emotional and spiritual self-care is needed to make life feel like it is worth living to you. If you are not thriving, you are not modeling thriving to your kids.

If you want your kids to believe that they can have happy and fulfilling futures, they need to see you happy and fulfilled. And you can't fake it. Kids see right through us. They are so well attuned to our moods and needs that they are constantly vigilant to our unspoken needs and desires.

If we sacrifice our emotional well-being for our children, not only will we not thrive, but it will not be good for our children. Being good to ourselves IS being good to our children.

The things that make you feel relaxed and happy are not indulgences or guilty pleasures. They are necessary components of a balanced life.

The most obvious sign that you aren't taking care of yourself well enough is when you notice that you are not the person you want to be or that you are engaging in toxic behaviors.

We all engage in toxic behaviors from time to time, so it is important not to shame yourself or attack yourself when you become aware of them. Think of them as a sign that there is something you need to deal with.

The four danger zones are the toxic behaviors: criticism, defensiveness, stonewalling, and contempt.

Criticism

When we criticize others, we verbally attack their personality or their character. This is different than giving feedback or holding someone accountable. This is about making them wrong in some way for being who they are.

The antidote to criticism is to state your complaints without blaming. To do this well, requires starting gently.

Arrange a time to talk. Ask if this is a good time. Present your concern as something you want to clear up because it is getting in the way of you being kind in the relationship. State the observable facts of the situation. Describe what the impact is on you. State what you need. Finally, make a specific request of the other person. When you are genuine in your desire to improve the relationship by dealing with this specific challenge, such complaints are generally better received than you fear.

For example, when a child has left a wet towel on the hall carpet, instead of grumbling, calling them sloppy, or complaining that they are so lazy they can't even be bothered to put their towels away, you should start by making sure they are listening and willing to participate in a conversation.

Once you have established that they are in the conversation with you, say something like, "I don't like being irritated with you because I don't like the way I talk to you when I am irritated, so I am hoping that talking this out will help. After your shower this morning, you dropped your wet towel on the floor in the hall. When I found it, it was time for you to catch the bus and I had to decide whether to put it away myself so you could be on the bus on time or ask you to do it and risk you missing the bus. I was irritated at having no good choices. Having to spend time dealing with that this morning, when I was already busy, added to my stress level and I felt disrespected. I need to feel respected and not like a servant to enjoy taking care of you. In the future, can you please hang your towels up on the towel hook in the bathroom after you have dried off?"

It can help to remember that your goal in making your complaint is not to exact revenge or cause harm. You are trying to avoid damage to the relationship, and you are willing to have this uncomfortable conversation to help the relationship.

When we complain, we are expressing the fact that

something about the world is not the way we want it to be. To take the toxicity out of complaining, it helps to acknowledge our sadness and disappointment and to recognize the dream or expectation we have been carrying around that has not been met.

Defensiveness

The second toxic behavior is defensiveness. Defensive behavior is a way of avoiding responsibility. We protect ourselves by blaming others. We often display righteous indignation or innocent victimhood. This is our attempt to ward off a perceived attack. It escalates the conflict by placing all the blame on the other person.

For example, when some parents are scared that they have failed to deal with a parenting situation well, they blame their kids for "making them angry." But the kids didn't make them angry. The parents got angry in response to a situation that included the kids.

The antidote to defensiveness is to accept responsibility for at least part of the conflict. A part of you feels responsible for something. If you didn't feel partially responsible and someone attacked you, you would be hurt or angry rather than indignant.

Almost all the time, when there is a conflict, each person contributes part of the problem. A conflict usually has more than one cause. It is the combination that created the problem.

Letting our kids see us take responsibility for our part in creating a problematic situation is an important part of teaching them how to handle conflict well.

It is possible to take responsibility for your part in causing a problem without excusing someone else's actions. You need to be willing to say, "This went wrong. I will take care of repairing the damage I caused, and I expect you to repair the damage you caused." If they respond defensively, you can stand firm, knowing that you are not being defensive. Their reaction is their responsibility.

Stonewalling

Stonewalling is the third toxic behavior. It involves removing yourself from a conflict and disengaging. People usually stonewall when they are emotionally flooded, overwhelmed, or triggered.

The antidote to stonewalling is to self-soothe. You must calm your physiological reaction to the stressful situation so that you can resolve it. If you cannot self-soothe without a break, negotiate a time-out.

Many parents retreat to behind a locked bathroom door for some deep breathing or emotional regrouping. Just make sure to tell your kids that you need to take a break to calm down and will be back to finish the conversation in a few minutes. Otherwise, your departure to self-manage may have the unintended consequence of increasing your child's stress.

It is important to negotiate your time-out rather than to abruptly take it. If you exit the situation abruptly, even to self-soothe, the impact on your child is the same as if you stay in the room and ignore them. In either case, they will feel the impact of your withdrawal. A well-negotiated time-out includes sharing why you are stepping out (to take care of your own emotional reaction so that you can communicate cleanly on your return), how long you will be gone, and a commitment to deal with the situation at a specified time.

It is also crucial that you continue the conversation after you have calmed down. If you do not return to the topic when you return, you will have effectively avoided the conflict and ignored the fact that your needs and their needs must be reconciled and some agreement reached.

The conflict will remain until it is addressed.

In the long term, you will want to reduce your need to withdraw in order to self-soothe. It is possible to be flooded or triggered and to stay in the conversation while self-soothing, but you may need to learn new skills and practice.

Many well-intentioned instructors teach people to pause, take a few breaths, and pay attention to what is going on in their bodies in order to self-soothe. Unfortunately, these particular techniques backfire for many people and create more anxiety and stress.

Most people find it easier to self-soothe without leaving a conversation using techniques that take the focus off themselves. Here are some things that you might find useful:

1. Focus on something the other person said or is doing that you are curious about. Ask them a question about it.
2. Think about someone you are inspired by and imagine what they would do in this situation. Try that.
3. Remember why the person you are in conversation with is important to you. What do you like about them when they aren't pissing you off?
4. What are you more committed to than your own discomfort? Focus on that.
5. Tell the person you are with that you are hooked, flooded, triggered, or overwhelmed. Sometimes just naming what you are experiencing releases its grip on you enough for you to stay engaged in the conversation.
6. See how the other person is expressing the attitude, feeling, or quality you think you need to get through the conversation and use your imagination to borrow it from them.

Practice these techniques when you are mildly irritated or slightly upset and they will get easier to use when you are feeling dangerously overwhelmed. It will take time to grow your capacity, but not as much time as you fear.

Contempt

The final toxic behavior is expressing contempt. Contempt is the sense that you are better than someone else. It is a form of hatred or disdain. Parents don't like to think that they might ever hate their kids, but it is surprising how easy it is to feel like we are better than our kids just because we have more life experience than they do.

Contempt often appears as a smirk, a snide remark, a condescending comment, or a sense that you know how to make them do something. It is important to remember, though, that we express what we believe in subtle ways even when we are trying not to. Contempt poisons even our best-intentioned actions if it is lurking underneath.

Contempt is dangerous because once you unconsciously decide you are better than someone else, you become less open to their influence, less willing to work through issues, and less willing to find compromises or alternatives in tough situations.

We know when people think they are better than we are. And it doesn't make us feel good.

The antidote to contempt is to create a culture of appreciation. Catch your children being good. Tell them how you see their strengths. Use sentences that start "What I appreciate about you is…" or "What I appreciate about that idea is…" You can appreciate ideas (or parts of ideas) that you don't agree with.

A subtle but powerful technique that helps reduce the presence of contempt is to use "and" to embrace what they have said while sharing your perspective.

For example, you can say, "What I like about that is that you get to be in charge of taking care of your own clothes and I worry that you will find yourself without clean clothes for school." This approach acknowledges that their desire and your concern exist simultaneously.

It would have a very different impact if you used "but." "What I like about that is that you get to be in charge of your own clothes, but I worry that you will find yourself without clean clothes for school." This sentence implies that your concern is more important that their desire and shows that you think you know more than they do.

Everyone shows contempt from time to time. It does not make you a horrible person. It makes you human. The first thing to do when you are starting to investigate your own contribution to a culture of contempt is to be kind and compassionate with yourself. What do you appreciate about yourself?

Don't be Afraid to Ask for Help

If you notice yourself falling into the danger zones, it is time to pause and focus on yourself with compassion and forgiveness. The trick is to catch toxic behavior quickly and change your behavior as soon as possible. Perfection is not possible, so do not beat yourself up for not achieving it.

Your commitment to continually improving your self-management is the key to coach-like parenting. It is sometimes hard work, but the pay-off is a healthy and mutually satisfying relationship with your children.

You may find you need to lean on friends or professionals to ground and center yourself when things get tough. Coaches, therapists, massage therapists, physical trainers, yoga teachers, and more might be part of your self-care team.

Asking for help when you need it is a form of wisdom, resilience, and strength.

You are worth it.

YOU CAN DO THIS

Parenting is hard.

No approach can make parenting easy. But a coach approach backed up by good self-care and your commitment to thriving while on this journey will remove the unnecessary burden of predicting the future and trying to do things that your children must do for themselves.

If this way of thinking about parenting is new to you, be gentle with yourself as you play with the new ideas. Try things out. Keep what works. You can only do what you can do. Your children are naturally creative and resourceful. They will find ways to compensate for your inevitable mistakes. Being disappointed by the humanity of our parents is a necessary part of the journey to maturity. You aren't messing your kids up by being less than ideal.

If you are surrounded by people who question your methods, find new people to support you. Get a coach. Find an online support group. Maybe there are programs near you that reinforce this approach. Buddy up with a friend to try things out. You are not alone in this work of parenting, even if sometimes it might seem that way.

All parents are making it up as they go along, following the leads of their children. Like everyone else, you are stuck balancing what you want to be able to do for your kids with the needs of running a household, maintaining your physical and mental well-being, keeping your relationships strong, and whatever you are doing to make a living. Of course, you feel like there is too much to do, not enough time, and more you could do for your kids if you only had the time. This is the reality we call parenting. It is a glorious mess.

On a personal note, I want to let you know that using this approach to parenting my own children has brought me an incredible amount of joy. I am honored and blessed to walk through the world alongside them.

I did not always feel this way. I used to feel responsible for their grades and their behavior even though I could not control it. I felt the pressure for them to perform to external standards, whether they were developmentally appropriate for my children or not.

Adopting this approach helped me manage my expectations and meet my children where they were. And they are thriving. Kids want to do well, and they do well if they can. Coaching helps us figure out what is getting in their way when they fail.

I wish for you to find ease, love, and joy along this challenging and rewarding journey. May you and your children flourish. May you see them soar and know that you provided the foundation on which they found their footing.

Happy parenting!

APPENDIX
EXAMPLES OF QUALITIES

Ambitious
Authentic
Brave
Capable
Caring
Coachable
Compassionate
Creative
Curious
Decisive
Determined
Diligent
Empathetic
Energetic
Fair
Fearless
Focused
Funny
Generous
Helpful
Humble
Inspiring
Intuitive
Inventive
Kind
Knowledgeable
Loving
Optimistic
Organized
Passionate
Persistent
Reliable
Resourceful
Sensitive
Supportive
Trustworthy
Visionary
Wise

ABOUT THE AUTHOR

Kate Arms, JD, CPCC, PCC, is the founder of Signal Fire Coaching. She teaches emotional, social, and relationship skills and offers individual, family, and team coaching. She works to create cultures where people are not only effective but happy.

She specializes in helping people navigate emotionally charged situations, manage emotional intensity and high-stress environments, balance multiple passions, and thrive despite struggles with anxiety and depression.

She writes about creating healthy interpersonal relationships at home and work, how to have effective high-stakes conversations, managing emotional intensity, building resiliency, and more.

She runs the *Thrive with Intensity* program and developed the Side by Side Model of Healthy Relationships.

Follow her online on Twitter (SignalFireKate), Facebook (KateArmsCoach), Instagram (SignalFireKate), and LinkedIn (KateArmsCoach) or at katearms.com.